Popular Education Practice for Youth and Community Development Work

Titles in the Series

To order, please contact our distributor: BEBC Distribution, Albion Close, Parkstone, Poole, BH12 3LL. Telephone: 0845 230 9000, email: **learningmatters@bebc.co.uk**. You can also find more information on each of these titles and our other learning resources at **www.learningmatters.co.uk**.

Popular Education Practice for Youth and Community Development Work

DAVE BECK AND
ROD PURCELL

Series Editors: Janet Batsleer and Keith Popple

LearningMatters

First published in 2010 by Learning Matters Ltd

British Library Cataloguing in Publication Data
A CIP record for this book is available from the British Library

ISBN 978 1 84445 207 1

Cover and text design by Code 5 Design Associates Ltd
Project management by Swales & Willis Ltd
Typeset by Swales & Willis Ltd, Exeter, Devon
Printed and bound in Great Britain by TJ International Ltd, Padstow, Cornwall

Learning Matters Ltd
33 Southernhay East
Exeter EX1 1NX
Tel: 01392 215560
info@learningmatters.co.uk
www.learningmatters.co.uk

FSC
Mixed Sources
Product group from well-managed
forests and other controlled sources
Cert no. SGS-COC-2482
www.fsc.org
© 1996 Forest Stewardship Council

Contents

Section 1
Theoretical background

Section 2
Practice

Section 3
Resources

Foreword from the authors

This book is for everyone out there who still wants to change the world. It provides a theoretical underpinning for community development and youth work practice which has as its aims individual and collective empowerment and social transformation. It equips students and practitioners to both critique and develop alternatives to top-down, social planning models by providing them with a range of analytical and practice tools derived from the work of Paulo Freire.

The book will provide students and practitioners with new and innovative ways to work with the National Occupational Standards for Youth Work and Community Development Work. It also introduces an alternative discourse to current policy debates: for example community regeneration, capacity building, social inclusion and the recent Community Development Challenge document from the Department of Communities and Local Government.

This book is particularly needed now as many contemporary examples of practice fail to deliver increased participation, community empowerment or sustainable social change.

Dave Beck and Rod Purcell
December 2009

Critical pedagogy

- All education is inherently political and all pedagogy must be aware of this condition.

- A social and educational vision of justice and equality should ground all education.

- Issues of race, class, gender, sexuality, religion, and physical ability are all important domains of oppression and critical anti-hegemonic action.

- The alleviation of oppression and human suffering is a key dimension of educational purpose.

- All positions including critical pedagogy itself must be problematized and questioned.

- Education must both promote emancipatory change and the cultivation of the intellect.

- Education often reflects the interests and needs of new modes of colonialism and empire. Such dynamics must be exposed, understood, and acted upon as part of critical transformative praxis.

Foreword from the Series Editors

Youth work and community work has a long, rich and diverse history that spans three centuries. The development of youth work extends from the late nineteenth and early twentieth century with the emergence of voluntary groups and the serried ranks of the UK's many uniformed youth organisations, through to modern youth club work, youth project work and informal education. Youth work remains in the early twenty-first century a mixture of voluntary effort and paid and state sponsored activity.

Community work also had its beginnings in voluntary activity. Some of this activity was in the form of 'rescuing the poor', whilst community action developed as a response to oppressive circumstances and was based on the idea of self-help. In the second half of the twentieth century the state financed a good deal of local authority and government sponsored community and regeneration work and now there are multi-various community action projects and campaigns.

Today there are thousands of people involved in youth work and community work both in paid positions and in voluntary roles. However, the activity is undergoing significant change. National Occupation Standards and a new academic benchmarking statement have recently been introduced and soon all youth and community workers undertaking qualifying courses and who successfully graduate will do so with an honours degree.

Empowering Youth and Community Work Practice is a series of texts primarily aimed at students on youth and community work courses. However, more experienced practitioners from a wide range of fields will find these books useful because they offer effective ways of integrating theory, knowledge and practice. Written by experienced lecturers, practitioners and policy commentators each title covers core aspects of what is needed to be an effective practitioner and will address key competences for professional JNC recognition as a youth and community worker. The books use case studies, activities and references to the latest government initiatives to help readers learn and develop their theoretical understanding and practice. This series then will provide invaluable support to anyone studying or practising in the field of youth and community work as well as a number of other related fields.

Janet Batsleer
Manchester Metropolitan University

Keith Popple
London South Bank University

Acknowledgement

We want to thank Kenny and Isobel from the Dopey Diner Cafe in Glasgow who allowed us to spend many hours drinking tea and planning this book.

Section 1

Theoretical background

Chapter 1

Why we need popular education: A critical review of current practice

CHAPTER OBJECTIVES

Youth and community development work has evolved over the decades. The way workers practice today is vastly different than from 50, or even 15 years ago. The development of practice is partly a response to what government and agencies believe works, and responses to changes in social conditions. However, it is also a reflection of the ideological position of governments and institutions which determine the policy and resources for practice; this has taken us to a place where current practice is largely ineffective. This chapter argues that there are fundamental flaws in current practice; hence the need for new approaches to which popular education can make a significant contribution.

The following histories of youth and community development work are intended only as a very brief summary to contextualise the discussion that follows. We have focused on the practice in the UK. In other developed countries the details will be different but the general points raised are likely to be applicable.

Youth work: A short history

Youth work practice in the UK has developed from a variety of activities, mainly for young men, in the mid to late nineteenth century: Sunday Schools, the YMCA and other initiatives focused on sports and social activities amongst the children of the poor. The Rev Arthur Sweatman, one of the leaders of this informal movement outlined his motivation for this work. He said, referring to young men:

> *Their peculiar wants are evening recreation, companionship, an entertaining but healthy literature, useful instruction, and a strong guiding influence to lead them onward and upward socially and morally; their dangers are, the long evenings consequent upon early closing, the unrestraint they are allowed at home, the temptations of the streets and of their time of life, and a little money at the bottom of their pockets.*

(Sweatman, 1867 quoted in Smith, 2002)

Towards the end of the century there was a parallel growth in provision for young women. Smith quotes the Girls' Friendly Society whose purpose was to *unite girls and women in a fellowship of prayer, service and purity of life, for the glory of God*. Also at this time religious-inspired uniformed organisations started to appear (Jewish Lads' Brigade, Catholic Lads' Brigade, Girls' Brigade and so on). Although often viewed these days as a conservative activity the Scouts and Guides were established by Baden-Powell in the early twentieth century as an educative venture to build fellowship and promote a sense of adventure for young people, in contrast to the regimented activities of the brigades.

Direct state promotion of youth began in the interwar period where local authorities were empowered to establish Juvenile Organising Committees. However it is not until the Albermarle Report in 1960 that youth work significantly moved from a voluntary and amateur activity to a state-funded and paid staffed service. The Report defined the youth work as offering

individual young people in their leisure time opportunities of various kinds, complementary to those of home, formal education and work, to discover and develop their personal resources of body, mind and spirit and thus the better to equip themselves to live the life of mature, creative and responsible members of a free society.

(Ministry of Education, 1960, p36, quoted in Smith and Doyle, 2002)

Even in this manifestation youth work was still primarily concerned with the young person as an individual, focusing on character-building activity and operating within the supposed consensual norms of society. Although issue-based and detached work did develop to some degree in the 1980s, this was as much a response to the decline in popularity and relevance of the youth club as a commitment to more radical conceptions of youth work practice. Jeffs and Smith (1990) amongst others have argued for a more focused and effective youth work service, but the overall range of provision and level of service performance could be said to be patchy at best.

In Scotland the Alexander Report of 1975 led to the integration of youth, community and adult education provision into a new local authority community education service, later reorganised as community learning and development. For many this has been an unhappy marriage. Youth work has tended to be the dominant partner, but the service as a whole has suffered from a consistent lack of clarity of purpose or method.

The Labour Governments from 1997 have refocused youth work as a service delivery operation as part of their social inclusion strategy. In England the Connexions Service attempted to unify services for young people through the transition from school to work period. Recent changes to the service have modified but not fundamentally changed this approach, with increasing emphasis on achieving outputs and meeting service targets.

Community development work: A short history

Community development has a similar history to that of youth work. In the UK it can be traced back to the urban Settlements such as Toynbee Hall in London and other major industrial cities during the latter half of the nineteenth century. Hall (1952) describes the establishments of the Settlements as recognising that *a society which truly seeks the welfare of its members is not only concerned that they shall live but that they shall have the opportunities for a more abundant life*. The movement accepted that many of the poor were victims of social change and believed that philanthropy and education provided a viable response. Like youth work there were few attempts at any systematic analysis of structural problems within society. The way forward was an individualised approach of enabling people to function within the existing social norms.

From the mid-1940s onwards a number of trends appear. The Ministry of Education produced a booklet extolling the virtues of community centres which stated: *Neighbours come together on an equal footing to enjoy social, recreational and educational activities either as members of groups following particular hobbies or on the basis of their common needs or interest as human beings living in the same locality* (quoted in Barr *et al.*, 1996a, p180).

At the same time community development workers from the ex-colonies were returning to the UK and bringing their methods with them. Their perspective promoted the ideas of participation, self-help within a normative framework and, crucially, a focus on very local contexts. The idea of restricting activity to a specific geographical area continues to operate in British community work practice. Partly this approach is due to the need to concentrate limited resources in areas designated as in greatest need. It also has the advantage from the government's perspective of limiting the analysis of needs and problems to particular estates. In this way overall structural analyses of social and economic problems can be sidestepped.

In 1968 the Gulbenkian Foundation reported on 'Community Work and Social Change'. The report identifies three main activities for community work:

- the democratic process of involving people in services that affect their lives;
- the personal fulfilment for those involved of belonging to a community;
- as an aid to community planning.

The report went on to stress the need to protect the interests of groups with special needs, especially in new communities, and for the redevelopment of 'twilight areas'.

Also in 1968 the Home Office established the Community Development Projects (CDPs). This was a response to a number of pressing political problems including what is known as the 'rediscovery of poverty' in a country that according to a Conservative party slogan *had never had it so good*, and increasing social tension in areas experiencing large-scale immigration from the Commonwealth.

A Home Office briefing stated that the CDPs were:

A modest attempt at action and research into the better understanding and more comprehensive tackling of social need . . . through closer co-ordination of central and local, official and unofficial, informed and stimulated by citizen initiative and involvement.

(quoted in Barr *et al.*, 1996a, p183)

The initiative was based on the then current US social policy of focusing provision on designated areas, with the emphasis on improved planning, local partnerships and re-including people back into the mainstream of society. This policy, with various adaptations and public relations faces, still underpins current governmental thinking.

During the time of the CDPs a variety of practices were developed, often reflecting the ideological position of the workers involved. Three main approaches to community development work were identified within the CDPs, which continue to underpin practice debates in the UK. These approaches are as follows.

- **Amelioration,** based largely around the Oldham CDP. The project accepted the view that only major socio-economic change could remedy some of the problems in the local project area. This being so, many problems could not be resolved. The Project team therefore adjusted its practical work programme to the local context and to largely self-help and ameliorative activities.

- **Traditional responses** where action was designed to effect changes *in the controllers of resources rather than in those who receive them*. The way to achieve significant change at the local level was to increase access to, and democratic control over, the resources that were already available. The operational goal was to radically change the organisation of resources within the local authority, not to act as an outside pressure group. Inevitably this method of practice leads to the involvement of local people into various manifestations of community planning and partnerships.

- **Radical responses** which rejected previous definitions of community work and attempted to evolve new forms more fitting with economic realities. The projects saw the interconnection between the problems encountered in the local project areas and the uneven nature of capitalist development. Rather than just accepting this as a given, or responding eclectically, these projects tried to develop along with input from effective local practices at the national level.

The radical group produced two major publications. The first, *Gilding the Ghetto* (CDP Inter-Project Editorial Team, 1977), argues that urban deprivation is not caused by the deprived themselves but rather that the problems of urban poverty were the consequence of fundamental inequalities in the economic and political system. Government development programmes were not about solving the problem of poverty but about maintaining the status quo and managing the poor. *The Costs of Industrial Change* (also 1977) argued that poverty was caused by unemployment through business decisions taken elsewhere, thus providing an early analysis of the effects of global capitalism on local communities.

This class analysis continued as an undercurrent in community work. Increasingly the feminist movement and workers operating within a Black perspective introduced a more critical awareness and ideological perspectives on gender, race, sexuality and ethnicity into radical community work practice.

By 2003 the National Occupational Standards for Community Development Work could outline the key purposes of the profession as being

- to collectively bring about social change and justice by working with communities to identify their needs, opportunities, rights and responsibilities;

- to plan, organise and take action;

- to evaluate the effectiveness and impact of the action.

. . . all carried out in ways which challenge oppressions and tackle inequalities (PAULO, 2003).

This is a laudable statement of intent; however, it was the amelioration approach and traditional responses which continued to dominate community work practice.

Practice in the 1980s and 1990s remained localised, and focused on a mixture of self-help and linking people into local planning processes. Community work became an increasingly professionalised and technocratic activity. This is illustrated by the market-leading community work textbook of the time, *Skills in Neighbourhood Work* (Henderson and Thomas, 1992, reprinted 2002). In this classic text, community work is seen as a series of steps: entering a community, identifying localised needs, setting goals, forming and building organisations, dealing with decision makers, and leaving.

In many ways the Henderson and Thomas approach reflects the strengths and weaknesses of current community work practice. These strengths can be characterised as: reflecting the reality that most projects have a local focus; understanding that social policies are area-driven; and understanding that many issues facing people manifest themselves in local neighbourhood issues and experience.

On the debit side of practice, and this would also be true of much youth work, is that the conventional practice model:

- ignores wider effects of globalisation, structural inequality, etc.;
- ignores the debates around feminism, identity, culture, sexuality, etc.;
- is weak on exploring the values underpinning practice;
- fails to adopt a rights-driven perspective;
- promotes models of participation where local people are largely powerless;
- draws people into establishment planning structures at the expense of developing autonomous and powerful local organisations;
- lights on any underpinning theory;
- accepts the political status quo (normative, communitarian);
- is based on an ideal of a mythical community;
- does not reach the approximately 2.5 per cent of the population (sometimes called the 'unreachables') who are in most need.

ACTIVITY **1.1**

Discuss the following questions.

1 *How far do you think the history of youth and community development work has shaped current practice?*

2 *Do you believe that current policy and practice is ideologically shaped?*

3 *Do you think the above critique of the limitations of current practice is reflected in your experience?*

It is important to be able to locate both your own practice and the practice of other organisations within this discussion in order to identify potential areas for collaboration and potential conflicts, for example, clashes of values or ideologies.

Some failings of contemporary practice

Contemporary youth and community work practice is a product of its historical development and the ideological position of policy makers. Henri Lefebvre (1991) suggests that the modern world is shaped by the created desire for consumption and the bureaucratic work, leisure and control structures that have been created to service this end. One of the results of this process is that our lives are no longer rich in experience. Instead we are organised on a daily basis according to the hegemonic needs of powerful institutions. In effect we are no longer *subjects* in control of our lives, and instead are *objects* to be controlled.

Despite the rhetoric surrounding youth and community work practice that suggests we are engaged in empowering people, much contemporary practice simply extends this institutional and bureaucratic control over people's lives. Embedded in this practice is what could be termed *the administrative approach*, which identifies needs according to statistical analysis plotted on maps to create supposed communities. From this analysis projects are developed, outputs specified and local workers dispatched to recruit and organise local people to the designated end. There is no doubt that some useful work is achieved through this approach. The problem, though, is that the opportunity costs are at the expense of local people exploring and defining their own needs effectively and the creating and sustaining of truly autonomous community organisations.

The administrative approach can be characterised as a sequential process as follows.

1　Create socially constructed categories of need; for example, 'social exclusion'. The categories are often labelled to defuse political analysis. 'Social exclusion' has generally replaced such terms as poverty or oppression.

2　Create socio-economic indicators to define it.

3　Collect statistics.

4　Plot the output on a map.

5　Draw a line around a concentration of these indicators.

6　Label this area a (dysfunctional) community.

7　Ignore the perceptions of the people who live in the area.

8　Establish local partnerships.

9　Recruit local people/community organisations to the partnership.

10　Make the 'community' responsible for solving the problems defined in 1.

Underpinning this approach to current practice is a fundamental misunderstanding of the nature of community. Although there is a lot of talk and some practice around the idea of 'communities of interest', the majority of contemporary practice appears still to be focused on locality and 'geographical communities'.

The centrality of geographical communities is underpinned by the work of Robert Park and what is called the Chicago School of Sociology. The Chicago School believed that effective urban planning and social intervention by agencies could improve the quality of life in cities. One of the current myths embedded in this approach is that if you live next to other people you have similar needs, interests and concerns, and that you will want to come together to respond collectively to issues raised by local workers.

Sometimes this is true and in the history of community activity there are innumerable examples of local people coming together over housing, roads, crime and safety issues. But these are often spontaneous responses driven by serious and immediate threats. The majority of community activity is far more mundane and does not have these unifying pressures and obvious collective interests.

CASE STUDY

Community integration

This case study relates to a research project commissioned by a local authority. The focus of the study was to explore the effect on a small town that was in the process of expansion through the construction of new private housing estates. The concern of the local authority was that the 'community' developing in the new estates would not integrate with the existing 'community' of the old town.

The old town had developed around the local coal-mining industry, which no longer existed. The Miners' Welfare Hall provided a focus to the area and organised the local gala, the main social event of the year. Research showed that a significant minority of the local population was involved with the miners' welfare in some way over the year.

There was no evidence that the old town had a single overarching community in any way. The research team identified many micro-communities. Usually these were based on extended family networks and relationships developed from school. These micro-communities tended to overlap in membership. However, this overlap was not sufficient to link together everyone living in the local area. Attitudes to the old town and desires for the future were varied; it was not possible to identify any commonalities of desires or concerns across the old town's population.

The new estates mostly housed people who had moved from the nearby major city. They tended to work in the city, shop at out-of-town malls, and have family and friends dispersed across the region. In effect many people on the new estates lived their lives across a wide geographical area. Contact with the old town and the existing population there was limited and was mainly focused on the primary school. There was little evidence that people on the new estates interacted significantly with each other.

The local authority wanted a formula that would enable them to understand how many new houses they could build before it became too difficult for the new community to integrate with the old community. The answer to their question was that not only were the new estates not a community in any functional sense, the old town was not a single community either. Integration, although a desirable policy goal, would not happen as there were not sufficient common interests and activities for this to happen.

Cohen (2003) argues that community is defined by *culture* and not *structure* as the Chicago School would have us believe. As Cohen put it, *community exists in the minds of its members, and should not be confused with geographical or sociographic assertions of fact.* That is you are part of a community if you feel you are part of it.

Geertz (1975) explored this idea, saying that *man is an animal suspended in webs of significance he himself has spun.* These webs of significance are based upon locating oneself within a community boundary and involvement in some kind of ritual activity which delineates the community members from non-members.

CASE STUDY

Glasgow Celtic

To illustrate this we can use the example of Celtic FC in Glasgow.

In this example the community boundary is the emotional allegiance to Celtic. The community are fellow supporters and the existence of non-supporters, and more importantly, supporters of other football clubs make this boundary more apparent. This feeling of belonging only means something through participation in ritual activity. Such rituals take many forms and in our example can include:

- *visiting the **symbolic home** – the Parkhead stadium – and ritual places (pubs, clubs);*
- *believing in an **underpinning mythology** – various conceptualisations of Irishness, republicanism, or being working class;*
- *understanding a **shared history** that may mean nothing to outsiders – Lisbon Lions, Jinky, Jock, Hendrik, etc.;*
- *participating in **ritual events** – Old Firm matches;*
- *wearing **ritual dress** – hoops;*
- *singing **ritual songs** – 'Walk On';*
- *participating in shared **'rhythmic muscular bonding'** (dance) – crowd performance;*
- *displaying shared **visual icons** – flags, colours;*
- *engaging in various **levels of participation** – season ticket, occasional attendee, TV watcher, or a vague emotional attachment.*

The Celtic FC community therefore is a community of interest that has specific geographical centres. Most communities are of this type. If we limit our focus to a fixed geographical area the situation becomes more diffuse and complex. Planners draw lines on maps and proclaim everyone within the line part of the same community. This is simply wrong. Just living in proximity to others does not, in the everyday course of events, lead to widespread interaction or shared interests. Our real functioning communities are based around workplace colleagues, leisure activities, family, and small groups of friends accumulated over the years. Within any given geographical area there will be numerous micro-communities based on the above; there is very likely no overarching sense or practice of community in any meaningful way.

Discuss the following questions.

- *Think about the geographical area where you live. Can you identify anything that everyone in that area is actively concerned about?*

- *List the micro communities to which you belong.*

- *Select one of these communities: what ritual activity do you engage in that promotes this community?*

Successful youth and community development work is based upon recognising and becoming involved with these micro-communities. A useful way of thinking about micro-communities is through the idea of social capital which enables us to understand why people come together.

Essentially, social capital is the name given to the networks that people belong to, along with the norms, relationships, values and informal sanctions that shape the nature and quantity of these interactions. Networks develop and are sustained if people trust each other and there is a feeling of reciprocity: I will help you, because you will help me. There are three main types of social capital.

1 *Bonding*: social capital between people who have similarities (e.g. among family members, people of similar age or within ethnic groups).

2 *Bridging*: social capital across different social groups (e.g. across ethnic groups).

3 *Linking*: social capital which crosses the gaps between social classes, the powerful/powerless, etc.

Robert Putnam (2001) argues that a healthy society has high levels of social capital (see also Field, 2003). Where there are high levels of social capital people:

- feel they are part of various communities;

- will participate in local networks and organisations;

- will help others in time of need;

- will welcome strangers;

- will help out with something (but no one will do everything).

Where social capital is high the task of youth and community development workers is made easier. The key to success is finding the pivotal figures in these networks. If the worker can make contact with these people, access to and the involvement of everyone in the network can often be achieved.

However modern societies, with the trends of social fragmentation and people living increasingly individualised lives, lead to reduced social capital and resulting social problems. Low social capital is often found when:

- there are low levels of trust between people, which in turn means that people do not engage with collective activities or networks and do not offer help to others;

- there are inadequate levels of material well-being – people are struggling for survival;

- there is inadequate physical infrastructure – such as places to meet, public spaces, telephones, newspapers;

- the human, economic and physical infrastructure pre-requisites are present but there have been no opportunities to develop the networks and interconnections between people.

In areas of low social capital the task of the worker is more difficult. One of the initial objectives for the worker is to help networks develop and to build trust amongst local people.

The need for popular education

Conventional practice takes the status quo and existing power relationships as normal. If youth and community development workers seriously want to engage local people in a process of personal and collective change, we need to see the everyday world in a more critical light.

Lefebvre (2008) argues that everyday life is not as it appears to be. We follow our daily rituals and accept the common sense view of right and wrong, what is true and what is good. As Foucault (1991) would have pointed out, although we take these ideas as fixed, they are simply social constructs created and disseminated by those who control society. Ivan Illich (2005) has also argued that the major institutions that significantly affect the quality of people's lives (and who often employ youth and community workers) usually operate out of self interest. Illich suggests this is true of schools, the health services and welfare agencies in general. He said:

> *Medical treatment is mistaken for health care, social work for the improvement of community life, police protection for safety, military poise for national security, the rat race for productive work. Health, learning, dignity, independence, and creative endeavour are defined as little more than the performance of the institutions which claim to serve these ends, and their improvement is made to depend on allocating more resources to the management of hospitals, schools, and other agencies in question.*

(Illich, 1973, p9)

Gramsci, as we discuss later, would have seen this process as a product of hegemony. Freire would describe the acceptance of this state of affairs as naive consciousness. Lefebvre, Gramsci and Freire all believed in the essential need to break down this mystification of life and understand our everyday experience in a more critical way.

Illich poses the question about social development and development work: is it about the consumption of more services and having access to more goods, or is it about changing how people live their lives and improving the quality of life? Current practice suggests the former, popular education stresses the latter. The task for workers wanting to promote change is to find ways to help develop what Freire calls critical consciousness.

Life in the modern world, suggests Lefebvre, is acted out in urban spaces such as streets, intersections, parks, community centres, pubs, and so on. These spaces are themselves socially constructed and reflect a dynamic mix of influences from historical legacy, local practices, globalisation, and so on. De Certeau (1984) maintains that these spaces are dominated by the powerful institutions of society which organise the use of these spaces in their own interest. He called this process one of 'strategy'.

In the main urban centres the effect of strategies can be strong. Overall, strategies organise our daily life, from going to work, and our time at work, through to leisure activities. In local estates the effect is less so and local interests may dominate how space is used. For example in a community centre the strategic power may be powerful members of the management committee, in a local park a local gang may be the strategic power after dark. In other cases local strategic interests may battle for control over space. Workers need to understand the dominant strategies in society and the local micro-strategies.

Modern life, say Lefebvre and de Certeau, is one of alienation. As a reaction to this people develop what de Certeau calls 'tactics' to try and make life more liveable. Tactics are mostly individualised and trivial, for example, taking extra time for lunch, surfing the internet at work, downloading films without paying, or avoiding the fare on the train. This is to be expected as we are living with naive consciousness and do not have a critical analysis of life. All we can do is make our own individualised response. In this context it is easy to blame others for your situation and see little to be gained from engaging in community activity.

The task for the youth and community development worker is to help people shift from this position of naive consciousness and individualised responses. To work with local people to develop tactics that critically explore people's experience of the world, collectivises issues, builds trust, reciprocity and social capital. The question is how to do this.

Lefebvre suggest that in everyday life there are times when *moments of vivid sensation* produce an insight into the nature of reality. He suggests art and carnivals can do this because they take us outside of the everyday experience. De Certeau wrote about assembling what he called creative imaginings that reinterpret the world view promoted by authority. This is a start but effective practice needs a more rigorous approach.

Popular education provides a rigorous process for enabling individuals to come together, to reflect on themselves, their place in the world, current needs and issues and to identify possibilities for change. Usually this process is seen as a cycle of Reflection – Vision – Planning – Action. The reflection phase is concerned with people reflecting on their lives, with the outcome a vision of how they want their life to be. From this vision planning can take place to enable action. Any action is then reflected upon and the process begins again.

We term the reflection-to-vision phase *'critical space'* as this is where people have to critically view themselves and society. There are a number of techniques to facilitate this reflection process. In classic Freireian practice it is through a listening survey to identify generative themes for analysis. However generative themes can be created and explored in many ways, for example, through art projects, video work, personal stories, poetry, and so on.

What is important is that popular education is seen as a method for critical reflection and social change. It is easy for the methods to be adapted to another end that does not attempt either. To be successful popular education needs to be rooted in the everyday experience of local people and to explore the overarching hegemonic process emanating from the state and powerful institutions. This book goes on to discuss how this may be achieved.

ACTIVITY **1.3**

Reflect on the following questions.

- *Think of an area (space) in the community where you work or live. What institutions and local interests have influence over what happens here? What strategies do they use to control the use of this space?*

- *Think about the tactics you adopt to make your daily life better. What is achieved by these tactics?*

C H A P T E R   R E V I E W

This chapter outlines the development and current limitation of contemporary youth and community development work practice. We have argued instead for a work practice that sees people as individuals not statistical objects, explores the nature of everyday life as it is lived, understands how life is controlled, builds social capital, brings people together and prioritises strategies to challenge the status quo and promote meaningful change. We suggest that popular education provides such a method.

FURTHER READING

Cohen, A (2003) *The Symbolic Construction of Community.* London: Routledge.

Cohen uses a wide range of anthropological examples to make the case for community being a cultural activity.

Field, J (2003) *Social Capital.* London: Routledge.

An excellent overview of social capital from a variety of perspectives.

Chapter 2
Social change

CHAPTER OBJECTIVES

This chapter explores some ideas around social change. This is an underlying concept of the value of *social justice* outlined in the National Occupational Standards for Community Work.

Social justice means:

- respecting and valuing diversity and difference;

- challenging oppressive and discriminatory actions and attitudes;

- addressing power imbalances between individuals, within groups and society;

- committing to pursue civil and human rights for all;

- seeking and promoting policy and practices that are just and enhance equality whilst challenging those that are not.

Similarly, it underpins the Key Purpose outlined in the Youth Work Occupational Standards (2008).

> Enable young people to develop holistically, working with them to facilitate their personal, social and educational development, to enable them to develop their voice, influence and place in society and to reach their full potential.

Although most youth and community workers and the agencies they work for would acknowledge that they are involved in the business of supporting and encouraging social change, their definitions of what that means are often superficial. As with many of the terms we are exploring in this book, *social change* is a contested term. It is therefore necessary for workers to think through their own position if they are not to waste their efforts on work which does not achieve meaningful social change. Social change is an inevitable feature of our lives. *The world is not finished. It is always in the process of becoming* (Freire, 1998, p72). The questions that remain for workers are: what the dimensions of social change are, what type of change is desirable, and what our role is in supporting those changes.

For the purposes of this chapter we will limit ourselves to consideration of intentional social change either for society as a whole or for particular groups within it since this is the type of change that workers are typically involved in. Naturally there are a whole range of social changes which are imposed on the communities and groups we work with. For example, at the time of writing there are massive changes affecting most communities in the world as a result of the global recession. Since these changes go far beyond the scope of most youth and community work practice these imposed social changes will not be the focus of this chapter. However, as we consider the dynamics of intentional change in this chapter, insights and principles may also be applicable to how we understand and work with those changes which are outside the control of workers.

ACTIVITY **2.1**

Think of a community group that you have knowledge of. Identify changes that have affected their work in the last few years and list:

- *the changes they have brought about themselves;*

- *the changes that have been imposed on them.*

What were the sources of these changes?

From this exercise you will see that there are a wide range of forces for change, some which can be influenced by workers and communities while others cannot. Whilst not losing sight of the bigger issues, community development starts with the issues which can be changed.

Social change theory

Clearly not all intentional social change is desirable. There have been many social movements which, either in intention or result, have produced very negative results for the whole or sections of society; we only have to think of the work of Pol Pot and the Khmer Rouge in Cambodia or Hitler in Nazi Germany to realise that this is true. Again, the assumption is that youth and community work practice should be about doing good and so the focus will be on intentional change which results in the good of society as a whole or communities within it. Of course the notion of what is 'good' is also a contested one and we therefore draw on the simple definition offered by James Coleman: an increase *in control over the conditions of existence or alternatively an expansion of resources* (1971, p61). The resources referred to would include finance, material resources, knowledge, networks, systems and influence, held individually or collectively, which enable a greater range of possibilities for the group.

Thin (2002) explores four themes of social change which allow the worker to interrogate their practice in terms of social change. They are:

- social justice: equal opportunity and the achievement of all human rights;

- solidarity: cohesion, empathy, co-operation and associational life;

- participation: opportunities for everyone to play a meaningful part in development; and

- security: livelihood security and safety from physical threats.

Any youth and community work practice which claims to be working for social change should be able to demonstrate specific impacts in some or all of the themes identified above.

ACTIVITY **2.2**

Think about the types of social change that you work for in your practice. What impact do these have on Thin's (2002) themes of social change (social justice, solidarity, participation and security)?

This typology gives a useful checklist with which you can assess the impact of your work. Not every project will achieve effects in all four areas but if it is not making a difference in any, can it still be considered to be effecting meaningful social change?

Coleman suggests that the main distinction in theories of social change are between those which start with changes in social conditions in which individuals find themselves and those that start with individuals themselves; from these theoretical positions flow two very different approaches to youth and community work practice. One seeks to change the material conditions that a group finds itself in and by so doing will increase its resources. The other focuses on individuals and develops their human and social capital which in turn would increase their resources.

Three foci of social change

In order to deepen our analysis of social change we must consider not just a general sense of things getting better, but identify the distinct arenas of social experience where intentional change for good can occur.

Legal change

One area of focus for youth and community work is in influencing law and social policy. There is a long tradition of community campaigning to change the law stretching back to the 1960s with CND and others. In recent years community-based campaigns around environmental issues, equality in marriage for same-sex couples, anti-discrimination, human rights, and changes in law and policy around asylum seekers have been to the fore. These campaigns have resulted in changes in law and in wider issues of social policy and have the ability to result in some aspects of social change.

An example of this type of change would be the Disability Discrimination Act 1995, an aspect of which made it unlawful for employers to discriminate against a disabled person:

- in the arrangements which they make for the purpose of determining to whom they should offer employment;
- in the terms on which they offer that person employment; or
- by refusing to offer, or deliberately not offering, that person employment.

The intention of the legislation was to increase the number of people with disabilities gaining employment, thereby achieving the social justice dimension of social change discussed above. Of course it is not quite as straightforward as that. Firstly, it could be argued that these legal changes are only a reflection of real changes that have happened in society rather than being the drivers of change. Therefore changes in the law have come about as a result of the campaigning work of disability rights groups and the resultant changes in societal attitudes.

However, legislation does enshrine these attitudinal changes and gives a clear basis to challenge any breaches. It could be similarly argued that legal changes are only effective when people have the power to enforce them. Again, in this instance it has been suggested that the legislation is made ineffective because individuals have to prove the case of discrimination against employers and that costs and other barriers put people off taking this action. It is further suggested that increased anxiety about costs for employers of making adaptations for disabled employees has in fact resulted in a reduction in the number of disabled people gaining employment.

And so while focusing on legislation remains a valid focus for social change it can be problematic, and cannot be expected to succeed on its own; parallel developments are also required in awareness-raising in the wider community and the development of power structures within communities experiencing injustice, which can then ensure that legislation is enforced.

It could also be argued that certain forms of government or constitutions will result in social change. In situations where there are authoritarian states the focus of social change could be the establishment of more democratic forms of power. Within the UK a legitimate focus for social change in which youth and community workers could be involved is the development of forms of democracy which are more participative than representational. Much of the work around community planning, for example, would fall into this category and would seek to fulfil the social change aim of developing participation and solidarity.

The role of community development is crucial in this arena, where social policy is outworked in practice since social policy often suffers from the distance between decision and implementation. We can all think of laws or policies which are good at the point of decision but fail at the point of the implementation, which are carried out by people and organisations who were neither involved in the decision nor support its aims, and are able sufficiently to amend, ignore or fudge it to rob it of any effectiveness. Youth and community workers are able to both work with the community to understand their rights and responsibilities and to organise to exercise control of the social realm and work with agencies and policy-makers to ensure that what was planned happens.

Economic change

The second area where youth and community workers can focus their efforts in achieving social change is what is broadly termed the economic sphere. These models of change are based on increasing economic resources in terms of actual money and free or subsidised housing, health, education and childcare, etc. with a view to moving groups and individuals from a position of low resource and dependence to high resource and independence.

Micro-finance initiatives give access to credit to the world's poorest people, which can then be used to establish businesses, take part in education or improve their homes and neighbourhoods.

CASE STUDY

Coin Street Community Builders

Coin Street Community Builders is another interesting example of how working on economic issues can achieve elements of social change. CSCB has transformed a largely derelict 13-acre site in the South Bank area in London into a thriving mixed-use neighbourhood by creating new co-operative homes; shops, galleries, restaurants, cafés and bars; a park and riverside walkway; sports facilities; by organising festivals and events; and by providing childcare, family support, learning, and enterprise support programmes (CSCB, 2009).

In the face of major office developments in the 1970s which would have decimated their community, local people formed the Coin Street Action Group. Seven years of campaigning, including two year-long public inquiries, followed. Eventually, the Greater London Council supported the community scheme. In 1984 the office developers sold their land to the GLC which, in turn, sold the whole site to Coin Street Community Builders.

All members of the company are required to live locally and so understand the needs and opportunities of the area. Their company is 'limited by guarantee' which means that it can carry out commercial activity but profits must be ploughed back into public service objectives rather than distributed to shareholders. Members have also set up a housing association and tenant-owned co-ops. Associated charities also support education, arts and community activities. Coin Street Community Builders works closely with neighbouring businesses and arts organisations.

The company continues to be financially viable due to the mix of housing, recreational and retail opportunities they have developed. Much of the revenue raising is a result of high-end restaurant and retail developments. The current director of Coin Street Community Builders says

> Unless as a social enterprise you are willing to cater for people with money, if you're only going to cater for people in poverty, you will never get to viability. Any strategy that is sustainable has got to have something which brings in money and recycles it – it's a Robin Hood approach.

(Bibby, 2001)

We can see from these examples that much can be achieved in terms of social justice, solidarity, participation, and security. However the results of this approach are not always guaranteed. It is suggested that individuals, communities or countries will be able to make use of these additional economic resources only if they have pre-existing *productive potential* (Coleman, 1971, p67). This is why the Grameen Bank focuses almost exclusively on working with women. They state that women are more reliable in paying back and that they use the loans more wisely than men (Grameen Creative Lab, 2009).

Similarly, the particular situation in Coin Street laid the foundation for the action that took place. Firstly, there were changed attitudes to authority exemplified by the rise of the consumer movement, CND and others. At the same time there were changes in planning legislation which ensured that the public had to be consulted as part of the planning process. Finally there was the social mix of the people involved in the campaign; these included local people, councillors, priests and workers – planners and community workers. It can be seen from that that the potential to take advantage of the situation was there and not all situations are as favourable as this one.

In conclusion, it seems that the immense possibilities for social change afforded by this approach can only be realised when they are based on a foundation of both the opportune moment and the mix of skills, experience and networks within the organisation taking up the challenge. The challenge for the youth and community worker is to both be able to read the signs of the times and to assess the capacity for groups and individuals to act in any given situation. To paraphrase Alinsky (1989), only take on battles you know you have a chance of winning.

Changes in individuals

Social change based on work which is directed at individuals is the final area to be considered. These are models based on the idea that social change is achieved by the aggregation of individual changes in beliefs, personality or lifestyle. These approaches can be broken down into two broad categories – individualist and revolutionary.

Individualist theories could be typified by an orientation towards achievement and a prioritising of the individual over the group – family, community. Social change is then effected by the aggregation of increases in individuals' human capital in the context of freedom from social constraint, and requires a stable market within which to operate.

Youth and community work approaches under this model would be typified by those focusing on the development of human capital and would include confidence building, training and skills development. The logic of this approach is that the development of skill and confidence can overcome the culture of communities which might be typified by lack of aspiration and limited expectation of meaningful employment. Increases in skills and qualifications would then lead to increased employment levels and more affluent communities. As a result of this, related issues of crime, drug taking, poor health, and so on would be improved.

A criticism that could be levelled at this approach is that, if the intention is social change in a neighbourhood, often what happens in reality is that individuals develop their confidence, skills and qualifications and leave the neighbourhood for a more affluent one. The result for a neighbourhood is detrimental because inevitably it is the more able members of communities who are able to make best use of these provisions. This is not to say that community-based education and training programmes are not valuable; clearly the impact of such programmes can be life-changing for the individuals involved. The problem does remain that these programmes alone may not achieve a collective change within the community. The challenge is therefore to consider what parallel interventions may lead to change on a community scale.

Perhaps it is useful to consider aspects of the other model of individual approaches which may add an important dimension to practice. Revolutionary theories posit change within individuals through taking part in the revolutionary act – it is the action itself which brings about the change. In contrast to the individualist view it is commitment to the movement rather than individual freedom and so social change is brought about by the collective force of the revolutionary group. Whilst not a revolutionary project as such, youth and community work approaches which have a strong campaigning focus can have some similar characteristics. Within these groups members re-conceptualise individual issues as collective issues, are united in a common cause to effect change within society and subsume their personal agendas in the overall cause.

Gittle *et al.*, in their study of women's Community Development Organisations (2009), indicate the potential of participation in collective action to achieve individual and social change.

> The participatory structure of most of the CDOs in our study and the way the organizations built participation into their programs created a democratic space where community residents could both form ties with each other and develop as individuals while collectively working for the betterment of the whole community.

(Gittle et al., 2000, p125)

There is perhaps an inherent instability within this approach because of the special conditions required to maintain the collective identity of the revolutionary group. For example, an organisation may be formed to campaign for improvement in housing conditions within a neighbourhood. This will result in a variety of collective and individual actions which will precipitate individual and social change; however, when the particular issue is resolved the group will either shrink dramatically in size or cease to exist.

CASE STUDY

Easthall Dampness Campaign

In the 1980s, residents of Easthall in Glasgow were living in damp housing conditions. Although experienced throughout the community, they had not previously made the connection between their living conditions, ill health and the social and environmental climate. The Easthall Dampness Group mounted a campaign to improve their living conditions. The local authority initially blamed the tenants, saying their lifestyle was the cause of the dampness. However the group became convinced that: 'It was not poor people who were to blame for the dampness but poor housing that was making the people poor' (McCormack, 1993, p209).

Over several years a coalition of local people and interested professionals researched, protested and lobbied for change – people who normally work independently from each other and who shared a common vision and interest, were brought together also to share and benefit from each other's expertise (McCormack, 1993, p211). The project was completed in 1992, resulting in flats which were super-insulated, with central heating, conservatory extensions, and the desperately needed clothes drying space.

Helen Martin (2008), chairperson of the Easthall Dampness Group, reflecting on the individual and collective impact of taking part in the dampness campaign observes that as well as achieving the changes in their housing conditions, being involved in this collective action had helped them to shift from a position of being naive (false consciousness) to becoming what Freire (1972) refers to as critically awake – the group could make the connections between the social, political and economic forces of power that determined and shaped their lives.

Challenges and tensions of social change

The work of Antonio Gramsci, particularly in his concept of hegemony – political and moral leadership exercised by one group over another – points to an essential inertia that must be faced by those seeking to effect social change.

> *Dominant groups in society, including fundamentally but not exclusively the ruling class, maintain their dominance by securing the 'spontaneous consent' of subordinate groups, including the working class, through the negotiated construction of a political and ideological consensus which incorporates both dominant and dominated groups.*

(Strinati, 1995, p165)

In this state people accept the prevailing order because they are compelled by the current apparatus of state and economy to devote their time to making a living and because they cannot conceive another way of organising society since they have internalised the vision and culture of their oppressor (Freire, 1972). They therefore fatalistically accept the world as it is, thereby rendering meaningful social change difficult. Social change in this context is therefore counter-hegemonic. It is not change for its own sake; rather, it seeks to replace an oppressive and dehumanising social order with a just one. Counter-hegemony suggests much more than merely improvement of material conditions, it must also contain elements of critical education (Allman, 2001) and the building up of networks of alliances between social minorities in order to develop a different consensus as to what society could be.

> *The revolutionary forces have to take civil society before they take the state, and therefore have to build a coalition of oppositional groups united under a hegemonic banner which usurps the dominant or prevailing hegemony.*

(Strinati, 1995, p169)

Within this collective process of social change, there is a role for exceptional individuals, described by Gramsci as Organic Intellectuals.

> *The mode of being of the new intellectual can no longer consist in eloquence . . . but in active participation in practical life, as constructor, organiser, permanent persuader and not just a simple orator . . . .*

(Gramsci, 1971, p10)

Brookfield (2005) argues that only indigenous leaders can truly fulfil this function since they alone can understand the people, feel their passions and therefore represent their interests. However we would suggest that youth and community workers, by virtue of their organic connections with groups and individuals within communities, have an important role in developing critical thinking and collective action in the pursuit of social change. They bring an understanding of processes of organisation and change, and theoretical ways of understanding social phenomena which can prove invaluable in enabling community groups to critically reflect on their lives and to plan, execute and reflect on action to change. We would argue that action which brings together local knowledge, global perspectives and clear theory and analysis will have a greater chance of achieving positive outcomes.

Even when a degree of success has been achieved, the battle is not over. Caroll and Ratner (2001) suggest that there are two challenges to maintaining counter-hegemonic activity. These come in the form of colonising and marginalising moves by both capital and state. Often organisations which cause trouble will have their funding cut, not be allowed representation on committees and generally be marginalised. If this tactic does not work, colonisation and incorporation is attempted. Many movements which start with radical intentions end up being drawn into 'the system' by being given buildings to run, staff to manage and service-level agreements to meet – thereby diverting them from their original mission and robbing them of their power to challenge the status quo.

In response to this, social action organisations must provide an ongoing basis for alternative formations of identity and community through a process of politicising their constituents and transforming received identity scripts. They must also provide an ongoing basis for alternative modes of satisfying the needs and nurturing the capacity of their community. Finally they must develop a repertoire of collective action that actively and visibly contests hegemonic relations and practices.

In conclusion, genuine social change is change that reshapes the balance of social power away from ruling elites into the hands of people who are marginalised in the current social order. It comes about through a process of critical thinking and collective action which produces people with a new vision of themselves and their society and new organisations which provide an abbreviated experience of transformed relationships and a power base for political change.

Ethical issues

Kelman and Warwick (1978) suggest that ethical issues must be considered in any social intervention, which they describe as *any act planned or unplanned that alters the characteristics of an individual or the pattern of relationships between individuals* (p3). They suggest four areas: the ends served by the change, the targets at which it is directed, the means of implementation and the assessment of the intended or unintended consequences. In each of these areas the worker must recognise the imbalance of power that could potentially result in their values and agendas being imposed on the community. As such this would be an act of *cultural invasion* (Freire, 1972) rather than an act of empowerment.

There is a difficult balance to be struck between a non-directive approach, whereby the worker might as well not be there, to one where the community group serves to act on the worker's pet projects. Neither of these extremes is desirable. Rather, problem-posing approaches must be sought which allow both the worker and the community group to enter into dialogue about the nature of the problem, its causes and solutions and appropriate ways to act to counter them. This process of co-investigation and collective action and reflection form the basis of an ethical and democratic approach to supporting social change. These are the approaches that this book explores.

C H A P T E R   R E V I E W

Youth and community workers are involved either in the business of social change or maintaining the status quo with all its inherent injustice and inequality. If, as we believe, people get involved in youth and community work because they want to make the world a better place, then a clear understanding of what social change is and how it can be best achieved is required.

FURTHER READING

Coleman, JS (1971) Conflicting theories of social change. *American Behavioral Scientist*, 14: 633–650.

This article discusses more fully some of the issues explored in this chapter. It provides people aspiring to be agents of social change a useful framework within which to create their practice.

Selinger, E (2008) Does microcredit 'empower'? Reflections on the Grameen Bank debate. *Human Studies*, 31(1): 27–41.

This article gives more information on the Grameen Bank debate.

Chapter 3
The legacy of Paulo Freire

CHAPTER OBJECTIVES

This chapter explores the historical background and key theoretical contributions of Paulo Freire. Firstly it examines the processes of education which either domesticate and maintain the status quo or liberate and promote social change. It then examines education as a cultural process. In particular, it explores *boundary situations*, which are the socially produced barriers which limit the potentiality of groups and individuals. Finally it examines how levels of consciousness can be developed to support collective social action.

Historical background

This brief biography draws on the very helpful work of Margaret Ledwith (2005) Denis Collins (1977), Peter Lownd (nd), Peter Mayo (1999) and the helpful Wikipedia entry which provides a useful starting point.

Paulo Freire is generally considered to be the most significant educationalist of the late twentieth century (Mayo 2004). He was born in 1921 in North Brazil to a middle class family and led a comfortable life until the depression of the 1930s plunged the family into poverty. It was here that Freire had his first experience of the impact of injustice and how it silenced people. Eventually the fortunes of his family improved and he was able to attend Recife University, where he studied law and philosophy.

After university he decided not to be a lawyer, but instead taught Portuguese. In 1944 he married Elza, also a teacher. As they began to work with poor people in Recife, Freire developed his ideas about the culture of silence; this also formed the basis for his doctoral thesis. He was then made chair of history and philosophy at Recife University. In 1961, as director of the Department of Cultural Extension at Recife University, he was able to demonstrate the effectiveness of his approach by teaching 300 sugar-cane workers to read and write in just 45 days. This resulted in the Brazilian government developing thousands of cultural circles across the country.

His radical approach to education was further developed when he was appointed as Director of Literacy, first in the north-east of Brazil and then for the national programme; his aim was to use literacy to raise political consciousness within the peasant class and to help them use their political power. However when the military coup took place in 1964 Freire was arrested and then later deported to Bolivia and then to Chile; he was not to return to his own country for 16 years.

Freire worked in Chile for five years for the Christian Democratic Agrarian Reform Movement and the Food and Agriculture Organization of the United Nations. In 1967 he published his first book, *Education as the Practice of Freedom*. He followed this with his most famous book, *Pedagogy of the Oppressed*, first published in Portuguese in 1968.

On the strength of the reception of his work, Freire was offered a visiting professorship at Harvard University in 1969. After a year at Harvard Freire moved to Geneva to work as a special education adviser to the World Council of Churches. During this time he acted as an advisor on education reform in former Portuguese colonies in Africa, particularly Guinea Bissau and Mozambique.

In 1979, there was an amnesty in Brazil, and Freire returned home in 1980. He joined the Workers' Party (PT) in the city of São Paulo, and acted as a supervisor for its adult literacy project from 1980 to 1986. When the PT prevailed in the municipal elections in 1988, Freire was appointed Secretary of Education for São Paulo. In 1986, his wife Elza died; he later married Maria Araújo Freire, who continues with her own educational work. On 2 May 1997, Freire died of heart failure.

Domestication or liberation

A Freirean approach to education is underpinned by some basic assumptions as outlined in *Pedagogy of the Oppressed* (Freire, 1972). These are the possibility of humanisation, the historical reality of dehumanisation, and a belief that dehumanisation occurs as a result of an unjust social order. This belief in humanity's potential to become more fully human gives rise to Freire's philosophy of hope and pedagogy of liberation (Ledwith, 2005). This approach then is neither one of empty theorising nor of meaningless action but a fusing of critical reflection on the world and action to change it, to humanise it, to make it more just. In this we can see there are clear parallels between this approach and the principles and values of youth and community work.

In order to effectively act to change the world it is necessary to understand the root causes of the injustice we see. Freire's understanding is that all social phenomena are produced by the complex interplay of opposing structural forces: labour/capital, rich/poor and oppressor/oppressed.

A further understanding which arises from this materialist analysis is that people's subjectivities are constructed by the complex relationships between themselves and their material conditions – their environment, social conditions and social relations. I worked with a group of women, many of whom suffered from depression and had low self-esteem. Some of them attended doctors who, taking an individualist approach, either gave them medication which made them feel a bit better or suggested counselling to help them cope. This approach again sites the problem in the individual and changes nothing in the wider community. I in no way want to devalue these as interventions but it seemed to me that their sense of who they were was a direct result of the social and material conditions that they lived in. They had poor housing, experienced poverty, had nowhere for

---

CASE STUDY

Two ways of working with under-age drinking

A local worker has observed an increase in drinking by under-age girls in the area she is working in. If she takes an individualist view she might come to the conclusion that these poor lifestyle choices are a result of lack of knowledge about the dangers of alcohol and develop a programme of information sessions to fill that knowledge gap. This approach both puts the blame on the individual and does not challenge any of the existing systems, attitudes and practices in the wider world. It also means that the expertise lies with the worker and not the group – they have not been given tools to analyse their lives and effect change.

If, on the other hand, she uses a structural analysis, she will pose questions about the causes of this social phenomenon, such as: how it relates to the economic structure of society, what the status of women is in this community and beyond, and whether there is any way that this behaviour serves the powerful and maintains the status quo. All of this would lead her to see that the drinking is a symptom of other forces in society and she would perhaps work with the young women to reflect on these and take collective action to effect some change. This is a more empowering approach as it allows the young women to analyse their lives and come up with their own solutions, it raises the possibility of change in oppressive structures, and it embeds a learning process both in the individual and in the group, so that further challenges can be dealt with without having to rely on the support of a worker.

---

the children to play, and had relationships with partners who were not always very supportive – no wonder they were depressed and had low self esteem!

The result of this more holistic understanding is, if you want to change the way that people think and feel about themselves and their world, you have to change their social and material conditions. In this case the result of that understanding of the causes of depression and low self-esteem was the development of a support group where women could talk and feel valued. This enabled them to experience different social relations and the confidence which flowed from that. They then went on to develop a range of play opportunities and campaigned successfully to improve their housing conditions. The results of this reflection and action were a beneficial effect on their confidence, happiness and hope for the future.

In all of this we can see that no education, youth work or community work is neutral – it either domesticates and shapes people to fit in and function within the given social order, described as 'banking education' or liberates causing people to act for change through critical analysis described as 'problem-posing' education. The educator must therefore ask *For whom and on whose behalf am I working?* (Mayo, 1999).

Banking education is described by Margaret Ledwith (2005) as an act of cultural invasion, involving the imposition of one's values, assumptions and perceptions of the world on others silencing and disempowering them. Freire (1972) describes banking education as:

> *An act of depositing, in which the students are repositories and the teacher the depositor. Instead of communicating, the teacher issues communiqués and 'makes deposits' which the students patiently receive, memorise and repeat. This is the 'banking'*

concept of education, in which the scope of action allowed to the students extends only as far as receiving, filing and storing the deposits. They do, it is true, have the opportunity to become collectors or cataloguers of the things they store. But in the last analysis, it is men themselves who have been filed away to the lack of creativity, transformation and knowledge in this (at best) misguided system. For apart from inquiry, apart from the Praxis, men cannot be truly human. Knowledge emerges only through the restless, impatience, continuing, artful inquiry men pursue in the world.

(Freire, 1972, p45)

It is extremely difficult for a worker to break out of this way of practising for many reasons. Firstly social policy lends itself to a top-down approach; government sets priorities and targets from which agencies establish programmes, and workers then have to find creative ways of engaging communities in those programmes. Secondly, it is very difficult for a worker to be aware of their own cultural assumptions and values which they unconsciously bring to their practice and impose on the people they work with. These are only exposed in genuine dialogue between workers and the people, which we explore in depth below. Finally, since people have been conditioned through school and other social experiences to be silent and to rely on experts to make decisions for them, they cast workers in this role and expect them to come up with the answers. This too must be struggled against through dialogue.

Freire's response to the approach described above, which only strengthens people's sense of powerlessness, is problem-posing education. This approach seeks to develop critical consciousness, a state where people see themselves and their lives in the context of their social reality and become capable of acting to change. They cease to be objects and become writers of their own story (Jesson and Newman, 2004). In contrast to the banking model of education where all too often information is 'crammed' for exams and immediately forgotten, within the process of dialogical radical education, knowledge becomes so well integrated and assimilated that it becomes located within our subjectivities, and thus, in addition to being known, it is felt, or subjectively experienced, as a type of lived compassion and commitment (Allman, 2001). And so it is a form of engagement which

---

CASE STUDY

A problem-posing approach to health is outlined by Mamary, McCright and Roe (2007). Using a technique called photovoice Wang and Burris (1997) explored the issue of sexual health with a group of non-gay identified African American men who have sex with men. Men within the group took photographs which represented aspects of the issue for them. These were then used as starting points for dialogues which identified what the key issues were and how they could be handled within that particular community.

Through this process they identified issues which challenged the way services are currently offered to men in this community, and also identified the strengths and assets within the community which allowed them to promote and maintain health. They report that the use of this technique helped to promote what Zimmerman (1995) refers to as psychological empowerment, the process by which individuals gain a sense of mastery over an issue of concern, take a proactive approach to life, and foster a critical understanding of the socio-political environment.

synthesises thinking, feeling and action which is located within the people and not just imposed by the worker.

Dialogue lies at the heart of this process of humanisation which we have been describing. This involves horizontal communication between equals involved in critical enquiry (Ledwith, 2005). Practically, it entails taking the thinking of group members and also the thinking as expressed in the 'knowledge object', as an object of collective focus, or reflection and concern, exploring why each person thinks as he or she does and where this thinking has come from (e.g. the historical and cultural context), and analysing whether it can enable the group to understand the world more critically. Although the starting point of dialogue is known the end point is not since it is the product of the group not the worker.

Until society itself is transformed, dialogic communication and learning will remain counter-hegemonic (Allman, 2001).

Education as a cultural process

Education, whether formal, informal or community-based is a potentially dangerous process. As youth and community workers, we bring our cultural values into the communities we work with; this is inevitable. The danger is, if we do so without reflection or criticism we will unwittingly impose our culture, thereby disempowering the very people we want to empower.

Freire describes this practice as *cultural invasion*. The process makes communities see reality through the eyes of the 'invaders', accept imposed norms and values, see themselves as inferiors and become powerless. This leads to a situation where people develop a Culture of Silence. In this state the world is named by others on their behalf, they feel ignorant, they become dependent and their knowledge and insights are less valuable than those of the 'experts'.

Before going on to discuss Freire's solution to this disempowering approach, let's look at an example of cultural invasion in action.

Much has been said in recent years about the centrality of the family for providing social stability and concerns have been raised about poor parenting skills leading to a range of social problems. Whilst much of that may be true, too often the response to the issue takes the form of cultural invasion. Firstly, initiatives based on middle class values and norms are generally focused on marginalised communities (Gillies and Edwards, 2006) and so, with good intentions, parents are reinforced in the idea that they don't know what they are doing and that other people are experts in their lives and not them. The result of this is an increase in dependence and an undermining of confidence in their ability to make choices in their own lives.

Freire's response to this approach is Cultural Action for Freedom. He recognises that culture is created through praxis – the integration of action and reflection – and that any cultural change must also be achieved through this process. He further stated that *boundary situations* are the starting point for change and that the goal is transformation of both personal and social reality.

Boundary situations

Taking up the same example, a youth worker talking parenting issues with a group of young parents might get the group to find images of parents and children from the media as a starting point. This might lead to discussions about their children's futures and they might come up with the idea that they are unlikely to get good qualifications and good jobs. This is the boundary situation. The worker would then help the group to explore all of the issues which keep that boundary in place – personal, economic, community values, schools, history, etc. – and think about ways in which they could effect change.

The benefits of this approach are that the issue of parenting takes its rightful place as one of a number of factors, parents are allowed to be experts in their own lives, and a range of action is identified which is collective as well as individual thereby building in the support needed for change.

From this example we can see that a boundary situation is socially constructed, feels very real to the person experiencing it, and yet can be changed through a process of critical thought and action.

ACTIVITY **3.1**

Think of a time when you were facing a boundary situation.

- *What were the factors – family, education, the media, peer groups, your personal situation, etc. – which led to the creation of this boundary?*

- *How did you feel in this situation?*

- *Were you able to overcome it? If so, how?*

- *If you were not able to overcome it, why was that and what did you learn through the experience?*

- *What does that teach you about working with people to overcome their boundaries?*

It is important to hold on to the feelings of working through our own personal boundaries. This will allow us to work sensitively with other people as we support them in their personal transformations.

Levels of consciousness

Finally, it is important for the worker to recognise the different levels of consciousness which people experience and what the implications of that are for practice. Freire talks about three levels of consciousness, Magical, Naive and Critical.

- *Magical consciousness:* In this state people are passive and accepting of their lot in life; their belief is that the situation is inevitable and unchangeable.

- *Naive consciousness:* In this state people recognise their personal problems but do not make the connection to wider social or structural issues.

- *Critical consciousness:* People recognise that the structures of society are unjust and the discrimination they produce affects them, the way they think and feel about their lives and the opportunities that are open or closed to them. This awareness leads to collective action for change.

It is clear from this analysis that only critical consciousness can support people to fundamentally change their world, and therefore youth and community work must incorporate mechanisms which help to lead to this state. Ledwith (2005) encourages workers to adopt practice which fosters curiosity, critical reflection, rigour and humility as means of revealing the truths hidden by ideologies and releasing people into action for change.

C   H   A   P   T   E   R   R   E   V   I   E   W

So we can see that Freire's legacy is a way of thinking about working with people which is applicable across many different contexts. The focus on questioning, rather than giving or accepting answers, helps the worker to be constantly open to change. The process of empowerment through the development of critical consciousness ensures that the relationship between the group and the worker does not become one of dependence. And finally, the understanding of power and the experience of freedom, gained by crossing boundaries, gives the potential to form groups and networks which are sustainable and support humanising social change.

FURTHER READING

Fritz, C (1982) *Because I Speak Cockney They Think I'm Stupid.* Newcastle: Association of Community Workers.

This book gives a great insight into Freire's approach in a community development context. It makes his ideas very accessible and gives the practitioner an insight into its potential in working with marginalised communities.

Freire, AMA and Macedo, D (eds) (1998) *The Paulo Freire Reader.* New York: Continuum.

This book features selections of Freire's work of the whole of his career; it is an excellent way to get a sense of how his ideas developed and matured over time.

Chapter 4
Gramsci

C H A P T E R   O B J E C T I V E S

This chapter explores the historical background and key theoretical contributions of Antonio Gramsci. It examines the ideas of *hegemony* and *counter-hegemony* as ways of understanding how society is shaped and conceptualising possibilities of social change. These ideas are linked to those of Freire and concepts of everyday life. Finally the chapter explores the nature of the organic intellectual as a way of recasting the role of youth and community development practitioners.

Understanding hegemony

Gramsci was born in Sardinia, Italy, in 1891. He joined the Italian Communist party and was for a time was its leader. In 1926 he was imprisoned by Mussolini. At his trial the prosecutor who clearly understood the power of ideas said: *"[F]or twenty years we must stop this brain from functioning"*. Whilst in prison Gramsci spent much of his time rethinking and writing about aspects of Marxism. His main concern was to explain why the Marxist prediction of a proletarian revolution had not happened. The core of Gramsci's ideas can be found in *Selections from the Prison Notebooks*. He was released in 1934 but died shortly afterward at the age of 46.

Gramsci's contribution to Marxist thought in particular, and our understanding of society in general, was to focus on how culture and belief are created and the ways in which this shapes collective and individual action. He believed that the predicted workers' revolution had not taken place because they had been socialised through the institutions of society (for example schools and the media) to accept a capitalist view of the world.

This world view embeds the ideas of individualism, aspiration to consumerism and a middle class lifestyle, and the 'natural' leadership role of ruling elites, the political mainstream and churches. By implication such a view rejects ideas of class analysis, collective action and radical/revolutionary change to the social order. In effect, Gramsci argued, the working class had been conditioned to accept a false consciousness about the nature of society. This false consciousness was so embedded in society and people's view of the world, that it was simply seen as 'common sense' or just 'how the world was'. Gramsci called this process of cultural domination, hegemony.

Such consideration takes us into the sociological debate around 'Structure versus Agency'. Put briefly, this is the question of whether the power of social conditioning and hegemony is so strong there is little people can do to overcome it, or whether people are able to reconstruct their personal and world view and act autonomously. Gramsci's view was that people are socially conditioned but that it is possible to overcome this through cultural action.

In Marxist theory there is debate about whether the conditioning process of the working class by the dominant ideology was *intentional* (planned and organised to this end) or *spontaneous* (a self-perpetuating reflection of the material structure of society). Gramsci was in the latter camp and argued that the hegemonic process was not a mass conspiracy by the ruling class nor a coherent and unified action. The policy and actions of governments would change as politicians and ruling political parties changed; various institutions of the state would all have their own agenda as would large corporations and small businesses. However, the differing messages were all variations of the political and economic status quo, because everyone thought their self-interest was linked to the maintenance of the existing social order.

To understand this more clearly we need to dip into Marxist theory on the *base* and the *superstructure* of society. By the base, we mean the way society is organised around the means of production. In contrast, the superstructure refers to everything that has been built on the economic base: social systems, culture, institutions, beliefs, etc. Marx believed that the nature of the base determines the superstructure. Having said that, he thought the superstructure would vary according to inherited historical influences, the degree of autonomy of various institutions and the diversity of social/cultural activity. Engels believed that a reciprocal process was involved here, in that the nature of the superstructure would also affect the way the base developed. Therefore the base and superstructure are part of an interlinking process that shapes society and the way people think.

Gramsci believed that this base/superstructure process did not automatically shape culture, but operated through a process he called *articulation*. Middleton (2002) suggests that the *theory of articulation recognizes the complexity of cultural fields* and that *it preserves a relative autonomy for cultural and ideological elements*. How this works out is through struggle as different classes fight to articulate culture according to their self-interest. In this sense culture becomes a class battleground fought through competing ideas.

The importance of ideas in shaping how people behave and creating the structures of society was further developed by Foucault (1991). He introduced the concept of *power-knowledge*. Foucault suggests that power is based on knowledge and the effective application of that knowledge to the real world. However, knowledge, according to Foucault, is not neutral. The way knowledge is constructed is ideologically based. History written by the ruling elite will be different from a people's history written from the perspective of the working class. Similarly, colonial history will be seen differently according to the position of the coloniser and the colonised. Social history looks different according to your gender or ethnicity.

The outcome of these positions is that power in society is essentially an ideological battle over the shaping of knowledge about the world – that is, a struggle between the hegemonic view of the world created by the dominant class and the counter-hegemonic view of the working class.

We need to remember however that Gramsci was a Marxist revolutionary and he was not interested in modest social reform; nothing less than the overthrow of capitalism was acceptable. The question was, given this analysis, what is to be done?

If the state and its allies promote social control through the hegemonic process the response must be through challenging this process; in effect a cultural war. Gramsci (1971) called this a *war of position,* where the objective would be to gain dominance in the media, education and other mass organisations to promote a counter-hegemonic message. Counter-hegemonic activity would challenge the perceived norms of society, heighten class consciousness and promote an ideal of a new society. Once the war of position had been won, then the *war of manoeuvre* or revolutionary takeover of society could begin.

The war of position would be promoted by *organic intellectuals*. Gramsci believed that all people are intellectuals, in that they have the capacity for rational thought. In capitalist society the role of the intellectual is limited to selected individuals with a specific hegemonic role: people who see themselves as a class apart and above the mass of society. To promote counter-hegemony what is required is a new cadre of organic intellectuals who would articulate the experiences and needs of the working class. They would also explore the dominant culture, to better understand the ideological position of the enemy. In addition organic intellectual activity would not only promote new ideas but would also organise debate and related action. As Marx (1845) famously said, *philosophers have only interpreted the world in various ways; the point is to change it*. The key to this process is for local knowledge to integrate with theory to form what is called praxis.

Gramsci did not wish to suggest that organic intellectuals were an elitist group. The intellectual as educationalist may have specialist knowledge, but so does everyone. He believed that organic intellectuals learnt from the experience of the working class and had a reciprocal relationship with them. Like Freire he recognised that true education is something that people do for themselves with the help of others, not something that is done to them by experts.

ACTIVITY 4.1

In a small group, reflect on your current practice and consider the extent to which each of you may be an organic intellectual.

The integration of knowledge and action are at the heart of the community development process. The ability to be able to both theorise at a high level and be intimately involved in the daily struggles of ordinary people is the challenge to the youth and community work practitioner. Without this integration we are left in the position, to paraphrase Freire (1972) of empty theorising or mindless activism.

Hegemony, everyday life and development work

It is important not to be reductionist in how we understand society. Although it is reasonable to argue that there is a hegemonic process generated through the everyday activities of the government, major institutions and business, the world is of course more complicated than that.

As we have said the institutions within society, whilst existing within the dominant framework of society, tend also to operate in their own sectional interests. This phenomenon has been explored by Ivan Illich (2005) in his writings about the health, education and welfare services. In effect institutions compete against themselves and, in doing so, open up spaces that can be exploited for promoting social change.

Michel de Certeau (1984) has also explored how institutions operate and their effect on the everyday life of individuals. He argues that institutions develop and promote *strategies* to extend their power over spaces, buildings, people and resources they directly control, and to influence wider social attitudes towards their products and activities.

In contrast individuals are concerned with making their life pleasurable, or at least reducing stress and uncertainty. Individuals take personal action all the time to this end and de Certeau called these acts *tactics*. This is often done unconsciously or emotionally, although it can also be a logically thought-out rational act. Tactics are mostly individualised and short term, and can range from minor action like taking a long lunch break to political activity. Whatever the scale of the activity they are in essence resistance to dominant forms of power. However, tactics may or may not challenge the hegemonic view of the world, and are more likely to be driven by false consciousness than promote critical consciousness.

What is important about the focus on everyday life and individual tactics is that it shifts the focus of analysis from solely what institutions do to people, to a more balanced view that incorporates how people respond to promote their own perceived interests. As has been said elsewhere, this represents a shift from people as objects to people as subjects. In this analysis people are to varying degrees autonomous players, rather than just victims of the powerful. This gives us a starting point to explore how counter-hegemonic activity can take place.

ACTIVITY **4.2**

Select an institution or agency of your choice. Explore how the users of their services are treated; are the users treated as objects *or* subjects? *What is your explanation for this? How far do individuals have* agency *(power to change their own lives) compared to the power of* structure *(conditioning to believe and act in a certain way)?*

Youth and community workers are clearly not in the business of a revolutionary overthrow of the state. They are in the business, according to the National Occupational Standards, of challenging oppression, promoting social justice and promoting empowerment. To do so involves changes in the distribution of power. As we have seen power is realigned through changing knowledge and this is essentially an ideological battle. It can be argued that any youth or community work that does not engage in ideological discussion about both the nature of society and the individual's understanding of the world will never effectively change anything.

Youth and community work is frequently engaged with local concerns, often in relation to activities of local authorities or institutions. Effective practice is therefore based on understanding the strategies of these institutions and the ideological basis of their activities. Work with local people here is about developing collective tactics of change or resistance underpinned by an alternative ideological perspective. Such a view of course problematises a lot of partnership work with local authorities where an unspoken assumption of ideological agreement underpins the partnership.

35

M11 Protest

This case study is based on the protests organised against the development of a link road to the M11 motorway in east London during the 1990s. Houses along the route had been compulsorily purchased. Some residents refused to leave and activists moved in, many with a radical environmental or counter-cultural background.

The drawn-out campaign was focused on Claremont Road, which became a centre for cultural activity, propaganda distribution, arts, music events and weekend parties, and a symbol of alienation and general discontent.

The protest was notable for a number of reasons.

- *It was a genuine co-operative effort between local people and external activists.*
- *Activities were effectively co-ordinated and enabled activities.*
- *There was a climate of freedom and creativity.*
- *It developed sophisticated approaches to getting the media on their side.*
- *It pioneered in the UK many of what have become standard tactics: roof top protests, media-friendly stunts, etc.*
- *It successfully (for a time) used the legal system. For example a tree house was legally designated a residence, thus blocking its removal by contractors.*
- *It made links between similar actions in the UK.*
- *It made the road protests a symbol of wider social discontent, around powerlessness, the power of developers, and general political malaise.*
- *It demonstrated that it is possible and often necessary to stand up and confront authority.*
- *'Direct tactics of resistance' were developed, based on building defences, tunnels, towers and barricades.*
- *Taking a longer term view: Claremont Road would be demolished but the costs and publicity involved would prevent further urban road building.*

Overall, what could be called the 'rainbow coalition' of interests and activities centred on Claremont Road and its re-creation as a 'temporary autonomous zone' was counter-hegemony in action. As one activist commented:

> No sign, relic or trace of Claremont Road remains. We always knew that one day all this would be rubble, and this awareness of impermanence gave us immense strength – the impossibility of failure – the strength to move this Temporary Autonomous Zone on to somewhere else. Our festival of resistance could never be evicted. We would continue to transgress the distinction between art and everyday life. We would continue to make every political act a moment of poetry. If we could no longer reclaim Claremont Road, we would reclaim the streets of London.

(Duncombe, 2002, p349)

Other activities of youth and community workers can focus on the individual: training for work, becoming healthier, or promoting mainstream social norms. All of this work should be subject to ideological debate (through a Freirean process). Such debates are essentially about exploring the hegemonic processes that have shaped the individual's view of the world and themselves and posing alternative futures. This work partly takes place through critical exploration of everyday life through discussion, reflection and the use of codes, but it also requires the exploration of external ideas and alternative lifestyles.

A further site of struggle is within the youth and community worker's own workplace. As already noted workers are often deployed to promote hegemonic ideas, to link community-based organisations into the power system of institutions and promote conformity to the status quo amongst individuals perceived to be deviant. Challenging the dominant ideological basis of this work and reframing the issue is difficult but an essential part of practice.

Whatever our employment or area of practice, we can always find spaces to contextualise our work in both historical and global frameworks. In addition we should, as Brookfield notes, use the power of cultural products (books, films, music, and theatre) as educational tools in this process. As an example he cites the work of Cornel West with black communities in the USA. In discussing the work of adult educators he suggests that the:

> *workplace learning programs, human resource development departments, non-profit agencies, and higher education, adult educators labor to create oppositional spaces in programs funded by corporations and government agencies. Such adult educators rarely have the luxury of aligning themselves with a movement or practice free of ideological manipulation . . . Instead this fight is a war of position. There is a nudge here, a push there, to bring the contradictions, tensions, and struggles from the world outside into their adult educational programs. Whenever adult educators temporarily displace themselves from ascriptions of authority and bring in 'ordinary' community members, rank and file activists, or grass roots organizers to play central instructional roles in a program, they are working in the organic way. . . . Similarly, whenever adult educators work to utilize critical theory's insights to illuminate the strategies and tactics that can usefully be employed in a particular struggle or movement, they are exemplifying West's prescriptions.*

> (Brookfield, 2004, p378)

Brookfield goes on to suggest that whereas Freirean practice is well thought out and has numerous guides on how to do it, Gramscian practice is more about having a distinct purpose:

> *A Gramscian adult educator has a clear sense of who the enemy is, and a sense of himself or herself as a directive persuader and organizer, rather than as a non-directive facilitator working to realize learners' agendas. Two adult educators who seem to me to work in this spirit are Michael Newman and Ian Baptiste . . . their intent to work in a partisan way is clear. Informed by a class analysis their understanding of the adult educator's role is of a directive catalyst who chooses to take sides and works only to further the cause of oppressed groups. This unequivocal commitment to taking sides and to allying one's efforts to those who have the least power in an unequal*

struggle seems to me to embody Gramsci's notion of the adult educator as organic intellectual.

(Brookfield, 2004, p380)

ACTIVITY 4.3

Discuss the following question.

Does youth and community work practice, where ideological issues are not discussed, achieve sustainable change:

- *for individuals?*
- *with groups?*
- *across the wider society?*

This is a difficult question for practitioners. Often we find ourselves in contexts where what we do is prescribed; however if we want to achieve change which is sustainable, we have to look for opportunities for critical reflection. This can happen no matter what the starting point may be.

A note of caution

Gramsci himself assumed that a critical analysis of dominant culture would lead to agreeing with the analysis of the revolutionary party. In post-modern times we now know that meaning is subjective and variable and that a fixed interpretation will not happen. This is as it should be. The agenda for discussion and the objectives for change should come from the person/group concerned. Counter-hegemonic work is not a recruiting exercise for a political group or for the worker to indulge their own political perspective. Being a concerned and committed worker is about facilitating others to create and explore their own agendas.

It is also important to recognise that people will only explore change when they are able to do so. Those in greatest need will be concerned initially with the basics of survival. For example there is little point in working with homeless people on an analysis of why homelessness exists until they have secured accommodation. Sensitively responding to people's needs is a fundamental aspect of good practice.

We need also to be aware that all ideas and methods are susceptible to be appropriated and used by people coming from differing ideological positions. For example Brenner (2006, p48) gives the example of the Christian/Republican right in the USA, from the late 1990s to the 2008 election, promoting a cultural message to convince the mass of the working population to accept individualist and religious fundamentalist policies, which were economically not in their interest, by playing on anxieties about race, threats to patriarchy and state control. In the UK, Margaret Thatcher won elections in the 1980s with a similar approach, playing on individuals' fears about race, unemployment and housing through blaming trade unions and 'liberals' for both imposing too much state control and undermining traditional values. These examples illustrate how cultural battles can be lost with the resulting reinforcement of false/naive consciousness just as much as helping people develop critical consciousness.

Freire and Gramsci

It is important to understand the differences and similarities between Gramsci and Freire. The following analysis is based largely on the work of Mayo and Brookfield. Both Gramsci and Freire come from a Marxist tradition so have an underlying common analysis that leads to many similarities in ideas. However, Gramsci was thinking about a Western European society in the 1930s, whereas Freire was writing about developing countries in the 1970s and 1980s. Marxism and social theory in general had changed significantly since Gramsci's time, so there are also differences in ideas.

Similarities

- All education is political, being based upon an ideological position.

- The ruling order will use coercion if necessary to sustain their power.

- Civil society is an area of conflict where cultural/educational processes need to change from dominant to transformational/counter-hegemonic discourses.

- There is a strong belief in the potential of human agency.

- Intellectuals/educators should be part of a process and learn from it, rather than experts who control it.

- The role of adult educators (and related workers) is to facilitate the challenging of the notion of 'common sense' and the everyday acceptance of how things are as being both right and inevitable.

- People should move from being *objects* that are controlled by institutions to *subjects* in control of their own destiny.

- The importance of *praxis* (linking knowledge to theory to action).

- Transformation through education will be most effective if linked to mass organisations and social movements.

- Local collective education – Gramsci through factory councils, Freire through cultural circles.

Differences

- Gramsci was concerned essentially with the traditional Marxist concept of the working class. Freire and broader Freirean practice identifies multiple sites of engagement around gender, sexuality, race and identity issues as well as the economic.

- Gramsci was interested in the conflicts between high (establishment) and low (working class culture). Freire is almost entirely concerned with exploring what he terms popular culture.

- Gramsci wanted a critical interpretation of history so the working class could understand the context of present society. Freire is mostly concerned with understanding the present and places less importance on the past.

- Freire believed that traditional teacher-led education (banking education) filled the student like an empty vessel. Gramsci thought that education was filtered by the individual's experiences and that all teaching was reinterpreted by the learner.

- Models of Freirean practice are well established, whereas Gramscian practice is more about intent and perspective than defined ways of working.

ACTIVITY 4.4

- *Gramsci said,* Telling the truth is always revolutionary. *Discuss with reference to youth and community practice. Revolutionary in what sense? Do you think Freire would agree with this?*

- *Explore the similarities and differences between Freire's idea of naive consciousness and Gramsci's false consciousness.*

A superficial reading of the literature may lead you to think that Freire and Gramsci are interchangeable. Whilst it is true that there is considerable overlap of their views, there are also significant differences. An exploration of these differences will lead to a greater insight to their arguments and their value to practice.

C H A P T E R   R E V I E W

This chapter has explored the basic ideas of Gramsci with respect to understanding how society operates through the creation of a hegemonic process. Gramsci argues that a response to this can be found through the creation of a counter-hegemony through the development of organic intellectuals. This idea has similarities with Freire and supports the ideas of Freirean practice.

FURTHER READING

Mayo, P (1999) *Gramsci, Freire and Adult Education.* London: Zed Books.

This book is an essential text for exploring the similarities and differences between Freire and Gramsci.

Illich, I (2005) *Disabling Professions.* London: Marion Boyars.

A classic critique of the interests and power of professionals.

Chapter 5
Youth and community work as transformational practice

C H A P T E R   O B J E C T I V E S

Youth and community work is a practice which seeks to bring about social transformation which is based on a set of values and principles. Without a clear understanding and application of these, community practice becomes an empty process which leads to tokenistic participation of people in the affairs of their life, thereby further disempowering the people it sets out to empower. This chapter explores some of those foundational values and principles and examines the way in which popular education practices give practitioners the tools to operationalise those values and principles. It pays attention in particular to *social justice* as cited in the Values and Practice Principles of Community Development (PAULO, 2003), and to two of the key roles of Youth Work (LLUK, 2008):

- ensuring that the rights of young people are promoted and upheld;
- promoting equality and the valuing of diversity.

Human rights

One starting point for anchoring community development practice is the issue of human rights. Jim Ife says that:

> A society that respects and values human rights is one where people are encouraged to exercise their rights, and accept a responsibility to do so where they can. This is an active participatory society, that requires citizens to be active contributors rather than passive consumers; and the promotion of such a participatory society has long been the agenda of community development.

(Ife, 2004, p4)

ACTIVITY **5.1**

Think of ways that youth and community work contributes to people participating in society. In what ways do these activities demonstrate respect for or uphold people's human rights?

A right can be defined as a special advantage that someone gains because of his or her particular status, a special advantage which gives access to a liberty, a power, an entitlement, or an immunity or a particular status by virtue of being a human being, a woman, a minority, an animal, a child, or a citizen of some country.

Ideas about human rights developed from seventeenth- and eighteenth-century natural law theories. For example Hugo Grotius (1625) expressed the notion of rights with the Latin term *ius*, a term that he also used to mean 'law', as in the phrase 'law of nature' (*ius naturale*).

Thomas Hobbes (1651) discusses the *right of nature*, which writers commonly call *ius naturale*. 'This is the liberty each man has to use his own power as he will himself, for the preservation of his own nature, that is to say, of his own life, and consequently of doing anything which, in his own judgment and reason, he shall conceive to be the aptest means thereunto'.

John Locke (1690) stated that:

> The state of nature has a law of nature to govern it, which obliges everyone; and reason, which is that law, teaches all mankind, who will but consult it, that being all equal and independent, no one ought to harm another in his life, health, liberty, or possessions.

Thomas Jefferson, in the Declaration of Independence, outlined this statement of human rights.

> We hold these Truths to be self-evident, that all Men are created equal, that they are endowed by their Creator with certain unalienable Rights, that among these are Life, Liberty, and the Pursuit of Happiness – That to secure these Rights, Governments are instituted among Men, deriving their just Powers from the Consent of the Governed, that whenever any Form of Government becomes destructive of these Ends, it is the Right of the People to alter or to abolish it, and to institute new Government, laying its Foundation on such Principles, and organizing its Powers in such Form, as to them shall seem most likely to affect their Safety and Happiness.

In the present day rights are usually discussed under the following divisions.

- **Positive rights:** Rights to benevolent actions from other people, such as rights to food, clothing, and shelter, or the right of an accident victim to be helped.

- **Negative rights:** Rights of non-interference; the right of an individual to pursue their interests without the interference of any individual or organisation.

- **Active rights** (rights to liberty): Rights to do as one chooses. For example, the right of movement entitles me to travel without being chained or locked up.

- **Passive rights:** Rights to be let alone, such as the right not to be injured, and the right to keep trespassers off my property.

As we can see a reliance on human rights as a foundation for practice is not as simple as it might first appear. Firstly one must ask which human rights we are referring to. Statements on human rights have been recorded throughout human history. The Declaration of the Rights of Man and of the Citizen, a foundational statement of the French revolution, was adopted in August 1789. More contemporary examples are: The American Declaration of the Rights and Duties of Man, adopted in April 1948 by the Ninth International Conference of American States in Bogota, Colombia; the Universal Declaration of Human Rights, adopted and proclaimed on 10 December 1948 by the

General Assembly of the United Nations; the European Convention on Human Rights, adopted by the Council of Europe on 4 November 1950; and the African (Banjul) Charter on Human And Peoples' Rights, adopted 27 June 1981 by the Organisation of African Unity. Not all of these can be considered Universal – applying to all cultures at all times – since, though these various pronouncements have similarities, they also have many fundamental differences. Given these competing claims for moral and political authority we must have ways of ascertaining their validity within the historical and cultural context within which we work, an issue which we will explore later.

Similarly, institutionalised human rights, both as a theory and as a social movement, has been widely criticised. It is claimed that it establishes Eurocentric political, economic, and cultural norms which it then seeks to impose on non-Western societies (Mutua, 2002). Marie-Bénédicte Dembour highlights a further five strands of critique of human rights theory.

- **Realists** *intimate that human rights cannot be 'above' or 'beyond' the state but necessarily originate from and are enmeshed within the state; they reject the idea that human rights are natural, existing outside of social recognition.*

- **Utilitarians** *oppose the granting of individual rights regardless of the consequences for the common good; nor do they think it is possible for human rights to be absolute and/or inalienable.*

- **Marxists** *view rights as sustaining the bourgeois order and thus feeding oppression by privileging a particular class to the detriment of the oppressed majority.*

- **Particularists** *object to the idea that moral judgements can be made which hold true across cultures; they call for tolerance of practices which are not comprehensible within the dominant perspective and denounce what they see as the inherent imperialism of human rights which are not universal but the product of the society which has created them.*

- **Feminists**, *finally, attack human rights' pretence of equity and neutrality by observing that rights, which have generally been defined by men, largely bypass the interests and concerns of women; they dispute the idea that human rights are gender-neutral.*

(Dembour, 2006, p4)

In addition to all of these theoretical concerns is the huge gap between human rights aims and the practice of the nation states that claim to uphold them calling into question their practical value. Despite the Universal Declaration being in place for over 60 years, Amnesty International (2008) states that *Injustice, inequality and impunity are the hallmarks of our world today. Governments must act now to close the yawning gap between promise and performance.*

What then is our response to human rights in the face of the confusing and contradictory picture outlined above? Firstly, in keeping with Community Development values we must see human rights as a collective issue. *Human rights become not so much a claim made by an individual or individuals, but a process and a structure for human community. From this perspective all humans share a moral order and are subject to moral law* (Ife and Fiske, 2006).

Human rights then, are collectively constructed, collectively understood and collectively experienced. I cannot have 'my' rights if you do not have 'yours', and hence they become 'our' rights (Ife and Fiske, 2006, p303)

ACTIVITY 5.2

Consider the following scenario.

The local neighbourhood centre has been approached by the British National Party who want to hold a public meeting about the UK's current 'immigration problems'. At the same time the local Asian community has approached the committee to say that they would be unhappy if the meeting went ahead because people from their community use the centre regularly and would feel intimidated.

If you were a worker there, how could you balance the rights of the BNP to freedom of speech and belief with the Asian community's right to freedom from fear – both of which come from the Universal Declaration on Human Rights?

This exercise begins to show the complex nature of human rights. These debates will always be contested and it is the debate rather than definitive answers that are useful to practitioners. Community groups should be encouraged to be involved in these debates rather than feeling that there are right answers which they must adhere to; this just stifles growth and sends dissension underground.

Secondly, also in keeping with Community Development values, we must see human rights as a bottom-up issue. This means that, rather than uncritically accepting an imposed set of standards devised outside the local community, which may not necessarily take into account that community's own values, culture and history, any statement of human rights becomes a starting point for critical reflection and action.

Finally, we must see human rights as praxis, not simply an idea to be considered or a set of actions to be undertaken by the powerful on behalf of the weak but the site for combined critical reflection and action which has as its starting point the experience of those who are robbed of their rights. As Jan Hancock puts it, *Moreover, the ideological pigeonholing of human rights as a hegemonic instrument rather than an arena of political struggle overlooks an important aspect of human rights as praxis; that is, as an instrument to challenge social power relations* (2006, p2).

ACTIVITY 5.3

This is an example of how to work with groups of people to explore the idea of human rights. It has been taken from Claude's Popular Education for Human Rights: 24 Participatory Exercises for Facilitators and Teachers (2000).

Step 1. *Facilitator input: explain that the Universal Declaration of Human Rights has 30 articles. One of its drafters, French scholar and diplomat René Cassin, said its many provisions could be seen all together as if they are the pillars of a temple holding up a broad roof. Each pillar supports human rights of a different kind. The first pillar is civil rights to*

ACTIVITY 5.3 *(continued)*

equality; the second social rights to protect the family; the third political rights for partici-pation; and the fourth economic rights for livelihood.

Draw a picture of a four-pillared temple and read Articles 1, 2, 7 and 8 from the simplified version below. Ask if they belong in pillar 1, 2, 3 or 4.

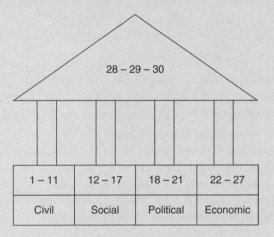

Figure 5.1

Step 2. *Ask if someone can name some political rights and then locate their answers for them among those in the UDHR below, for example, the rights noted in Articles 18 to 21. Ask for similar examples of social rights, for example those found in Articles 12 to 17. Follow the same or varied procedure to elicit the economic rights linked to the fourth pillar and found in Articles 22 to 27.*

Step 3. *Facilitator's short lecture: explain that one drafter of the UN Declaration of Human Rights, Charles Malik from Lebanon, felt strongly that all these rights focusing on the individual needed something more to hold them all together – a roof to rest on the four pillars of the temple and to interconnect them all together – saying that these rights must be supported worldwide with all countries cooperating to promote human rights. Malik explained that the last three articles are very broad in order to overcome the other-wise biased view that rights are largely negative – that is, rights to be protected from state interference and things which governments must not do, such as interfering with freedom of the press. He wanted to include in the UDHR the view that governments, alone and in international combination and cooperation, have duties to implement a favourable national and international social structure within which human rights can take root, and that international duties also call on prosperous states to assist the economic development of poorer states. Articles 28, 29 and 30 try to set out principles to harmonise rights, that is, that they must not be exercised in ways conflicting with other UN objec-tives – for example, free speech should not be misused to disseminate war propaganda and so on. In other words, the last three articles of the UDHR (28 to 30) seem to say, we need a roof to hold it together. Do you think these articles embrace everybody worldwide in responsibilities to hold things together?*

ACTIVITY **5.3** *continued*

Step 4. *Have participants count off: 1, 2, 3, 4. Everyone numbered 1 will form the civil rights group, all 2s the social rights group, 3s the political rights group, and 4s the economic rights group. Group 1 should report back their answer to the question why civil rights (Articles 1–11) stand for My right to be me. Group 2 report why social rights (Articles 12–17) carry the banner: Don't interfere with us. Group 3 report why Articles 18–21 have the slogan I can help decide. Group 4 report on economic rights in Articles 22–27 and why they support the claim, I need work and a livelihood.*

Step 5. *Ask people from Group 1 to name a few civil rights. Then ask others in Groups 2, 3 and 4 how it would affect the rights they have discussed if the rights named from Group 1 were abolished. Repeat this for various rights so as to show, for example, that if the political rights pillar is destroyed, other pillars will fall, or that if economic rights are ignored and violated, social and civil rights will suffer. Open a general discussion to see if participants understand that all human rights are interconnected. Remove one pillar and the temple will fall. Does this show that all rights are important parts of a whole structure, or do people think that some rights are more important and some can be ignored without undermining the others? In general discussion, see if participants appreciate a holistic notion of human rights.*

Appendix for Activity 5.3
Universal Declaration of Human Rights – Simplified Version

Civil rights

1 *All human beings are born free and equal. We are all the same in dignity and rights and have the same rights as anyone else. This is because we are all born with the ability to think and to know right from wrong, and so we should act toward others in a spirit of friendliness.*

2 *Everyone should have the same rights and freedoms, no matter what race, sex, or colour he or she may be. It shouldn't matter where we were born, what language we speak or what religion or political opinions we have, or whether we are rich or poor.*

3 *Everyone has the right to live, to be free and to feel safe.*

4 *The buying and selling of people is wrong and slavery should be prevented at all times.*

5 *No one should be put through torture, or any other treatment or punishment that is cruel or makes the person feel less than human.*

6 *Everyone has the right to be accepted everywhere as a person, according to law.*

7 *You are entitled to be treated equally by the law, and to have equal protection of the laws.*

8 *If your rights under the law are violated, you should have the right to have fair judges who will see that justice is done.*

9 *You should not be arrested, held in jail or thrown out of your own country for no good reason.*

10 *In case you have to go to court, you have the same rights as anyone else to a fair and public hearing by courts that are open-minded and free to make their own decisions.*

11 *If you are blamed for a crime, you should be thought of as innocent until you are proven guilty. You shouldn't be punished for something you did which was not illegal when it happened.*

Social rights

12 *No one should interfere with your privacy, family, home or mail, or attack your honesty and self-respect without a good reason.*

13 *Within any country you have the right to go and live where you want. You have the right to leave any country, including your own, and return to it when you want to.*

14 *You have the right to seek shelter from harassment in another country.*

15 *No one should take away your right to live in the country you come from.*

16 *Grown men and women have a right to marry and start a family, without anyone trying to stop them because of their race, country or religion. Both have to agree to marriage and both have equal rights in getting married, during the marriage, and if and when they decide to end it.*

17 *Everyone has the right to have belongings that they can keep alone or share with other people, and no one should take your things away without a good reason.*

Political rights

18 *You may believe what you want to believe, have ideas about right and wrong, and believe in any religion you want, and you may change your religion if you want without interference.*

19 *You have the right to tell people how you feel about things without being told to keep quiet. You may read the newspapers or listen to the radio, and you have the right to print your opinions and send them anywhere without someone trying to stop you.*

20 *You have the right to gather peacefully with people, and to be with anyone you want, but no one can force you to join or belong to any group.*

21 *You have the right to be one of the people in your government by choosing them in fair elections where each vote counts the same and where your vote is your own business. Because people vote, governments should do what people want them to do.*

Economic rights

22 *As a person on this planet, you have the right to have your basic needs met so you can live with pride and become the person you want to be; other countries and groups of countries should help.*

23 You should be able to work, choose your job, join a union, have safe working conditions, and be protected against not having work. You should have the same pay as others who do the same work. You need decent pay so your family can get by with pride, and that means that if you don't get paid enough, you should get other kinds of help.

24 Everyone has a right to rest and relaxation, and that includes limiting the number of hours required to work and allowing for a holiday with pay once in a while.

25 You have a right to have what you need to live a decent life, including food, clothes, a home, and medical care for you and your family. You have the right to get help from society if you're sick or unable to work, or you're older or a widow, or if in any other way you can't work through no fault of your own.

26 You have a right to education. At least in the early years it should be free and required for all. Later education should be there for those who want it and can undertake it. Education should help people become the best they can be and to respect the human rights of others in a peaceful world.

27 You have the right to join in and be part of the world of art, music and books, so you should enjoy the arts and share in the advantages that come from new discoveries in the sciences. If you have written, made or discovered something, you should get credit for it and get earnings from it.

Community responsibilities

28 Everyone has the right to a world where rights and freedoms are respected and made to happen.

29 We all have a responsibility to the place where we live and the people around us, so we have to watch out for each other. To enjoy freedom, we need laws and limits that respect everyone's rights, meet our sense of right and wrong, keep peace in the world, and support the United Nations.

30 Nothing in this statement means that anyone may weaken or take away our rights.

National Occupational Standards

Both community development work and youth work have nationally agreed standards. The National Occupational Standards for Community Development Work (2003) outline the purpose, roles and values which guide practitioners.

Community Work Standards

Key purpose

The key purpose of community development work is collectively to bring about social change and justice, by working with communities to . . .

- identify their needs, opportunities, rights and responsibilities;

- plan, organise and take action;

- evaluate the effectiveness and impact of the action;

. . . all in ways which challenge oppression and tackle inequalities.

Roles
The roles of community development work are to:

- develop working relationships with communities and organisations;

- encourage people to work with and learn from each other;

- work with people in communities to plan for change and take collective action;

- work with people in communities to develop and use frameworks for evaluation;

- develop community organisations;

- reflect on and develop own practice and role.

Values
The key values of community development work are:

- social justice;

- self-determination;

- working and learning together;

- sustainable communities;

- participation;

- reflective practice.

Youth Work Standards

Similarly, youth work has its own set of National Occupational Standards (2008):

Key purpose
Enable young people to develop holistically, working with them to facilitate their personal, social and educational development, to enable them to develop their voice, influence and place in society and to reach their full potential.

Values
- Young people choose to be involved, not least because they want to relax, meet friends, make new relationships, to have fun, and to find support. The work starts from where young people are in relation to their own values, views and principles, as well as their own personal and social space. It seeks to go beyond where young people start, to widen their horizons, promote participation and invite social commitment, in particular by encouraging them to be critical and creative in their responses to their experience and the world around them.

- It treats young people with respect, valuing each individual and their differences, and promoting the acceptance and understanding of others, whilst challenging oppressive behaviour and ideas.

- It respects and values individual differences by supporting and strengthening young people's belief in themselves, and their capacity to grow and to change through a supportive group environment.

- It is underpinned by the principles of equity, diversity and interdependence.

- It recognises, respects and is actively responsive to the wider networks of peers, communities, families and cultures which are important to young people, and through these networks seeks to help young people to achieve stronger relationships and collective identities, through the promotion of inclusivity.

- It works in partnership with young people and other agencies which contribute to young people's social, educational and personal development.

- It is concerned with how young people feel, and not just with what they know and can do.

- It is concerned with facilitating and empowering the voice of young people, encouraging and enabling them to influence the environment in which they live.

- It recognises the young person as a partner in a learning process, complementing formal education, promoting their access to learning opportunities which enable them to fulfil their potential.

- It safeguards the welfare of young people, and provides them with a safe environment in which to explore their values, beliefs, ideas and issues.

Complementary purposes

Let us then consider the complementary purposes of community development work to 'collectively to bring about social change and justice' and youth work to 'enable young people to develop their voice, influence and place in society' and how popular education practices provide a methodology to achieve these ends.

Margaret Ledwith (2005) points out the danger of losing sight of the radical nature of youth and community work which leads to amelioration rather than change; in other words, the danger of becoming part of the problem rather than part of the solution. Popular education puts groups of people and their felt concerns rather than prescribed programmes at the heart of the process. Taking seriously the issues and concerns of people is the first step in an empowering process. It locates people as the experts in their own lives and gives them the opportunity both to reflect on their current situation and its causes and to think and plan for a better future. Rather than giving people solutions it poses problems for people to solve.

Larry Olds (2007) provides a useful template for planning interventions which ensure that these principles are embedded within practice.

- Start with experience.

- How do the activities help people name their world, tell the stories of their experience, speak and find their voice at the educational event?

- Deepen analysis and add new information and theory.

- How are tools of social analysis used to help people connect their experience to a broader understanding of it, to understanding political and other social connections?

- Involve the whole person – the artistic voice.

- What activities will be used that use art, music, theatre, dance, and other ways to use people's non-verbal capacities?

- Try to become more fully human.

- What activities will be used to develop consciousness about becoming more fully human as well as to develop consciousness about the world?

- Confront oppression and privilege.

- How will you address race, class, gender, sexual orientation and gender expression, culture and other issues of privilege and oppression?

- Work with, not for, people.

- How will you address the teacher/learner – learner/teacher issues?

- Apply to action.

- What will be the links between education and action?

- Respect people's knowledge.

- How does the activity advocate a people-/community-centred versus a banking approach to knowledge?

C H A P T E R   R E V I E W

It is clear that popular education practices provide ways of working which both take seriously the human rights issues experienced by marginalised communities and work with the principles and values of youth and community work. These are by no means simple issues to work with; rather, they call for reflective practitioners who understand the subtlety of how power works and how change can be effected. Neither does popular education consist simply of a collection of techniques; instead it requires commitments on behalf of the worker. A commitment to social justice is obvious but as importantly a commitment to submitting to an ongoing process of collective reflection and action in order to become more fully human. A realisation that we are not the finished article and that none of us knows anything fully may seem like a weakness but is in fact the strongest foundation youth and community workers can have.

Claude, RP (2000) *Popular Education for Human Rights: 24 Participatory Exercises for Teachers and Facilitators.* Cambridge MA: HREA.

This free-to-use training manual outlines highly participative activities which can be adapted and used in a variety of youth and community contexts.

Ife, J (2004) *Linking Community Development and Human Rights.* Deakin University, Australia: Community Development, Human Rights and the Grassroots Conference.

This is a useful article examining the parallels and commonalities between a community development approach and a human rights approach and suggesting that one can strengthen the other.

Chapter 6
Global popular education

CHAPTER OBJECTIVES

In this chapter we explore what is understood by transformational practice in a global context. We note that although there are different cultural interpretations, it is possible to identify underlying themes that are reflected in Freirean practice. The chapter then explores a number of case studies to illustrate the diverse ways that popular education can be practised. We also suggest a number of related group activities and follow up reading.

What do we mean by transformational practice?

Transformational practice is based on a number of core ideas. At a macro level it is of course about responding to social issues through promoting change. At an intellectual level transformational practice is concerned with questioning the nature and validity of knowledge. At a personal level the transformation is about helping us to learn and grow in a holistic rather than fragmented way.

Macro level

In their classic text *Training for Transformation* (1984), Anne Hope and Sally Timmel explore meanings of transformation. In particular they categorise the different nature of responses to poverty and levels of awareness that apply to popular education. The table below combines and amends their work.

ACTIVITY 6.1

- *Reflecting on your own practice, where would you locate yourself in this table?*
- *Where would you want to be?*
- *If there is a difference, how do you account for it?*

Table 6.1

	Magical/naive consciousness	Naive to limited critical consciousness	Critical consciousness
Type of change	Functional Non conflict	Functional Limited conflict	Structural Conflictual
Definition of the problem	Fate	Education deficit Culture Alienation Exclusion	Structural oppression
Value base **Approach**	Charity Paternalistic	Self help Enabling with boundaries	Challenging oppression Facilitating
Goals	Relieve suffering	Develop self-reliance	Build alternative structures and processes
Programmes	Relief Welfare Care services	Technical training Credit/money advice Employment creation	Co-operatives Workers councils Social movements Trade Unions
Type of leadership	Top down Non-participative	Consultative	Participative Shared responsibility
Type of activity	Welfare	Development	Liberation Transformation

We must recognise that critical consciousness is a process not a destination; we must continue to reflect, challenge and be challenged by others in order to maintain a critical perspective.

Intellectual level

Carolyn Clark (1993) has explored the intellectual aspect of transformation in an influential article that draws on the work of Mezirow (1989) and Daloz (1990) as well as Freire (1972).

The first question is, 'What does it mean to be human?' Essentially this is about being able to have control over our actions as a rational and autonomous adult. To live in this way implies a level of critical thought and a relative degree of freedom to act. Such action has to be based not on personal and selfish interest, but as a reflection that we live in a world of social relationships and are also dependent upon the actions of others.

The second question is, 'How do we know something is true?' Our interpretation of the world is subjective; what an event means to us is different to the meaning of it for other people. Clark quotes Daloz: *As human beings, we are active participants in the process of making meaning, of constructing ways of knowing the world that help it cohere in a way that makes sense for us* (Daloz, 1990, p8). How do we develop a common and critical understanding of the world we live in?

This takes us to the third question, 'What is the relationship between the individual and society?' For change to take place based on collective action it is important that we begin to create a common understanding of the world. The Freirean process explored in this book is designed to do that through exploring locally based collective experience, and collective critical interpretation of that experience.

ACTIVITY **6.2**

How do we know something is true?

Go as a small group to a local shopping street (a railway station, art gallery or similar location will work as well). Individually, explore the area and make notes on the questions below.

Questions:

- *Who is there – what assumptions can we make about their class, ethnicity, occupations, etc.?*

- *What are they doing?*

- *What does this activity tell us about the place?*

- *How do you feel about being here?*

Meet and compare observations, discussion common perceptions and differences.

Account for the differences of opinion: are they based on personal experiences and interests, different age/ethnicity/gender, different ideological positions, or something else?

It is important at this point to remind ourselves again not to fall into the trap of playing the expert. In particular as we are thinking about global examples of practice, to recognise that different cultures understand and experience knowledge in different ways.

In Western cultures knowledge is assumed to be provable, written down and objective (i.e. that it is out there and not something personal and internal). Activity 6.2 shows that this assumption about knowledge is significantly incorrect and that in the West we should open ourselves to exploring knowledge from different points of view.

Personal level

Sharan Merriam and Young Sek Kim (2008) have explored non-Western forms of knowledge and suggest that we could usefully analyse it from several perspectives.

Their initial point is that in traditional non-Western cultures *learning is communal*. Not only that but one's own identity is not as an individual as in the West, but is based on the notion of collective identity. In effect, events, and our experience and understanding of them are the product of the collective interactions between people. This is illustrated by Burkhart.

> *In Western thought we might say that my experiences and thoughts count more than your experiences because I have them and you cannot. But if we are WE, then this constraint seems rather trivial. The hand may not have the same experiences as the foot, but this hardly matters if we understand them not as feet and hands but as this*

body. If it is through the body, or the people, that understanding arises, then no one part need shape this understanding.

(Burkhart, 2004, p26)

In this context the purpose of learning is not for personal gain but for improving the well-being of the community through the sharing of knowledge and collective and reciprocal activity.

Secondly, *learning is both lifelong and informal*. Lifelong learning in the West is usually posed in a fragmented way. For example it can include vocational education to get a better job, extra-mural or evening classes to pursue personal interests. Often this is termed as learning for its own sake, and is based around taught classes and devoid of any real purpose or follow-up activity. Of course we learn daily in a variety of informal ways, but our understanding of learning has been shaped so that we only value it if it is a product of a course or certified in some official way.

In non-Western cultures lifelong learning is understood as an informal process that is embedded in everyday experience and necessary to enable the individual learner to improve their contribution to society. Much important informal learning is created through problem-solving activities based around daily life.

Thirdly, non-Western cultures believe that *learning is holistic*. In the West learning is seen as something that takes place through and in our minds, and as we noted above learning is fragmented; it is something from a class, from a book or maybe from television. Although we learn all the time through daily experiences, by not recognising or valuing this, the lesson and benefit is lost.

For non-Western cultures learning is an integrated process that takes place through the mind, the body, emotions and the spirit. Although this is an integrative process, it is also important that all four aspects are balanced. Alongside mental growth, it is essential that our bodies are fit, our emotions are balanced and our spiritual side is met. This learning is rooted in the experience of daily life and through participating in rituals and collective experiences.

The alert reader will have noted that the Freirean process does all these things. It explores the questions of what it means to be human, critically explores what is true, collectively links people together to explore social issues, valourises informal learning and promotes a broad and integrated notion of the self.

ACTIVITY 6.3

Think of an experience where you felt strong emotions. This could have been a very happy experience or a situation where you felt threatened or upset. Only pick a situation which you feel comfortable sharing with other people.

In a small group share your experience and consider the following questions:

- *What did you feel?*
- *How did these feelings affect your behaviour at the time?*
- *How did these feelings affect your behaviour subsequently?*
- *Did you consciously learn anything from that experience?*
- *Do you think that experience unconsciously modified your behaviour?*

Inner city youth education (Noguera, 2007)

One of the questions frequently asked about using Freirean theory in practice is how relevant it is in contemporary urban communities. This study responds to that question by looking at the experience of young black males in New York who are in prison, or at risk of going to prison, mainly for street crime and drug-related offences.

The study describes how the young men in the study possessed what Freire calls 'submerged consciousness'. This means they create their own interpretation of the dominant ideology as the best way of surviving life in a poor community; in this case through selective violence, gender oppression and aggressive strategies to make money, in this case selling drugs. Gramsci would have said this was an example of how hegemony operates to promote activity that in reality is counter-productive to the objective needs of the people concerned.

Noguera points out that in order to undertake any effective work it is necessary to understand the social and psychological environment in which the young men live. In effect it requires time and skills to become involved in the local culture, and to some extent be seen as acceptable to it. Only when this has been achieved can listening surveys be undertaken and generative themes determined. Inherent in this is developing an understanding of why these young men engaged in crime and violence, and the logic of such activity for them (understanding this logic is not the same thing as condoning or colluding with it).

The breakthrough with the group came in a discussion about whether it is acceptable to give drugs to your sister. The answer was clearly no. The next question was whether it was all right to sell drugs to your friend's sister. The answer was yes, because that's business. This led to a long discussion on the effects of drugs, boundaries of friendship, the effect of drugs on the community, and, eventually, how they had found themselves in this position. It was then possible to explore alternative life strategies. This process only worked because Noguera had developed acceptance amongst the group; they would not have engaged in this process with an outsider.

In reflecting on the work Noguera poses important questions about the nature of Freirean practice. He rightly points out that Freire's dichotomy of the oppressed versus the oppressor, although effective in establishing the basic premise of the work, oversimplifies the position. The young men were clearly oppressed in terms of class, race and the effects of unemployment and poverty. However, they were also oppressors of young women and those who were dependent upon their drugs. The dual positions that we can find ourselves in and the contradictions that this entails has to be acknowledged. There is no point just seeing the young men as victims of oppression as this will only create a one-dimensional understanding of a complex social situation.

A second point is that it is easy to slip into believing that a purely educational strategy will empower people. Developing a critical consciousness changes our understanding of the world and our place within it; it does not actually change any of the structures and practices that create social injustice. Hence the importance of stressing that we are concerned with transformational practice, not simply an educational process. Critical consciousness needs to lead to collective action.

`CASE STUDY`

Cuba – Popular education transforms women's lives (Acosta, 2007)

Felicia Pérez's experience is an example of the impact that popular education has had on the daily lives of Cuban women, whose potential for self-realisation is often repressed by the dominant machismo of Cuban men, or who are belittled if they devote themselves to home-making work. Felicia commented that popular education taught me that every person has knowledge, and deserves respect. . . . I learned that everyone has value, and now I don't feel inferior because I'm a home-maker.

Felicia brought together a group of women in a low income area of Guantánamo, Cuba. Initially the group met for handicraft classes. For many women it is necessary to start with such activities, partly due to the self-defined boundary limitations of the people concerned, sometimes due to restrictions put on the women by their male partners. All the women are of post-retirement age and were previously domestic workers. Felicia herself was at the time of the group's formation in her mid-sixties. To help them develop the group, contact was made with the non-governmental Martin Luther King Jr. Memorial Centre (CMMLK) who assisted them to learn and apply popular education methods.

In the group setting the women discuss a range of subjects related to health, sexuality, the family, and the history of their city and its colonial and postcolonial history. The group is part of a larger project known as Celia, whose remit is to address the lack of knowledge about architectural treasures and the lack of citizen and urban culture . . . and to attract women and talk to them about the city and its history, so as to foster a sense of belonging *(Acosta, 2007). However, once a popular education process begins, the journey that people are engaged in often takes them far beyond the initial remit.*

A number of personal changes can be identified as developing from the popular education practice and there is now a Network of Popular Educators in Cuba. Iluminada Brizuela has spoken about a radical change in the family and working life: I'm a different person, my self-esteem is much higher, and the way I communicate with other people has changed . . . before, if my husband told me not to go out to the government food store, I wouldn't go. Now, he washes the clothes, irons, cooks and looks after our daughter.

Brito, another popular education participant commented: This approach is not the one true way, but it is one of the ways that can work effectively, like a grain of sand in the building of better things for our country.

Participation and education in the Landless People's Movement of Brazil (McCowan, 2003)

The Landless People's Movement of Brazil (MST) is widely known for the scale of its operation and the number of people involved. It is essentially an agrarian reform movement, which has established a network of schools in its communities. The schools and the educational process they promote are based on principles of social justice to be implemented through the creation of a radical democracy. The purpose of the educational process is overtly political as it seeks to equip landless peasants with the skills and knowledge to enable them to become effective players in the wider society, effectively empowering education for change. The MST has won over 15 million acres for land reform, and established more than 1,500 agricultural communities, providing an income for over 250,000 families.

The MST believes that people will only fully believe in, and act in accordance with, democratic principles if it is a lived experience. This practice must start within education. Decision making begins at grass roots level and works its way upwards. Realistically, decisions cannot be made by everyone so the MST has a policy of participation and the division of tasks according to the question at hand. This is in direct contrast to much contemporary community development practice where decisions are made by statutory bodies, communicated downwards and local people recruited to implement them.

Education is seen by the MST as a political activity. McCowan offers the following quote:

> This school is the product of the struggle. It's not here because the government wanted it here; it's here because the families marched in Salvador and struggled and finally got it. Everything you see in the settlement is the product of the struggle.

> *(McCowan, 2003)*

Furthermore, education operates from the position that people exist within particular set relationships, which are themselves a product of a social and historical context. People therefore, have individual needs but this has to be understood and responded to through collective responses. Unless this is understood and acted upon, education will fall back into the traditional mode, seeing the person as an isolated individual.

Related to education is the idea of citizenship. MST believes to be an active citizen it is necessary to have an education to understand what is required and your role in it. Citizenship requires both an understanding and claiming of rights, followed by the exercising of these rights. To do so effectively requires critical consciousness.

McCowan describes how the following structures are found within MST communities:

> The general assembly is composed of all the members of the community, meets once or twice a year and discusses and approves the overall plan for the school as well as other significant or controversial matters.

> The education team is composed of a representative number of teachers, pupils and community members and meets monthly. Here the details and implementation of the overall plan are discussed. Like all MST nuclei, the community representatives are

chosen by direct vote by the community as a whole and are accountable to the general assembly. The pupils are generally chosen by their classmates, and all the teachers are normally represented.

The teachers' collective involves all the teachers, and customarily meets once a week to organise the day-to-day running of the school, including lesson-planning, special activities and the 'generative themes' (cross-curricular topics of study).

The pupils' collective organizes those tasks for which the pupils have responsibility, such as the school pharmacy, meals or assemblies. It also provides suggestions on the general plan of the school as it affects the students. The age of the representatives and the selection procedure depend on the individual community.

It has to be recognised that for some this is not the way to organise education. Many parents feel it is not their responsibility to become this involved with what they see as the teacher's job, or dislike the political overtones of the process. It can also be unclear how much decision-making power younger pupils do, or should have: can they over-ride the will of the teachers, should they? There also appears to be evidence that for participation to work, the traditional inequality related to gender has to change. The MST themselves recognise the enormity of such a cultural change and that they have a long way to go to achieve functioning gender equality.

(McCowan, 2003)

CASE STUDY

Theatre of the Oppressed Laboratory (Picher) (see also Chapter 9)
The project is based in New York and both performs and promotes the methodology of the Theatre of the Oppressed as developed by Augusto Boal. This work is undertaken by a group of educators, cultural and political activists and artists. They work with educators, human service and mental health workers, union organisers, neighbourhood, peace, youth and rights organisations.

Marie-Claire Picher writes of the project:

The principal goal of popular education is to change the power relations in our society and to create mechanisms of collective power over all the structures of society, so too the principal goal of the Laboratory is to help groups explore and transform power relations of domination and subjugation that give rise to oppression.

Within this learning process:

1 all participants are learners;

2 all participate in and contribute equally to the production of knowledge, which is a continuous dialogue;

3 the learners are the subject and not the object of the process;

CASE STUDY *continued*

4 the objective of the process is to liberate participants from both internal and external oppression, so as to make them capable of changing their reality, their lives, and the society they live in.

(Picher, undated)

The project has organised intensive workshops led by Augusto Boal, and has delivered over 200 workshops in a range of sites including community locations, public schools, colleges and universities. The workshops help organisations explore their self-defined issues and explore ways forward. Examples of work include:

• *the role of the arts in the struggle against racism;*

• *building solidarity among women living in shelter accommodation;*

• *AIDS prevention and promoting health among homeless people with HIV/AIDS;*

• *a teach-in on Confronting Right-wing Ideology and Social Policy;*

• *working with indigenous communities, offering training workshops for social justice workers and educators including training peace and social activists;*

• *working with street children in Mexico City;*

• *working in El Quiche, Guatemala, in conjunction with health and literacy educators, women's rights groups, and community organizers;*

• *working in Guatemala City with psychologists and teachers of at-risk pupils.*

The work of the project relates directly to organising for democratic social change, to explore how people see themselves, to propose and achieve solutions to collective issues through democratic group processes. This involves developing support structures, building confidence and capacity of participants and growing leadership skills.

C H A P T E R R E V I E W

This chapter has discussed interpretations of what can be understood by transformation practice in a global context, and its relationship to Freirean practice. Some of the themes have been illustrated through case studies.

FURTHER READING

Clark, C (1993) Transformational learning. *New Directions for Adult and Continuing Education*, 57: 47–56.

A recommended article to begin to explore questions around the relationship between the intellect and transformation.

For more insight to emotional learning and emotional literacy a good place to start is Goleman, D (1996) *Emotional Intelligence: Why it can matter more than IQ*. London: Bloomsbury Publishing.

Section 2

Practice

Chapter 7
Overview of how groups work

CHAPTER OBJECTIVES

Youth and community activity usually takes place within group settings. The NOS for both youth work and community development work reflects this, and group work is explicit or implicit across the standards. Effective group work practice is essential to being a successful practitioner.

This chapter explores how groups work and how to develop effective learning within a group setting. It also discusses the relationship between group work and development activity. Finally, we explore the importance of understanding the inherent power relationships within groups.

Effective practice

As social creatures we are naturally members of groups all the time. For example, Henderson and Thomas (2002) suggest that people may join community-based groups in order to:

- protect their personal and/or family interests;

- support social and cultural activities;

- improve the quality of life within their community;

- preserve or create community assets;

- examine opportunities or repel threats, whether real or perceived.

In the youth and community field groups are created by workers for a variety of purposes. These purposes include:

- for leisure and recreation;

- to socialize normative behaviour in children;

- to modify behaviour in (under-functioning and deviant) adults;

- as therapy;

- for creative or artistic ends;

- for development objectives;

- for management or team building objectives.

Select a group – it can be an education class, a youth group, community group, or another relevant to you. Think about how the group is organised, the power relationships in the group, and how gender, ethnic and sexual issues are dealt with. Does the process involved promote or reduce equality?

Apart from work-related groups we seldom think about our relationships as group processes at all, and our participation in and understanding of them is usually implicitly accepted. As is the case with Freirean practice it is important to make unconscious behaviour both conscious and reflective. Across all of the above categories there are choices to be made about values, principles, and indeed the very purpose of the group. To make this clear we can conceptualise groups according to a series of choices. Groups can be:

Didactic (top down)	or	Socratic (shared discussion)
Formal (committees)	or	Informal (responsibilities are shared)
Office-bearers control activity	or	Collective responsibility
Valuing conformity	or	Valuing difference
Reinforcing norms	or	Challenging oppression
Inward (focused on the group)	or	Outward (focused on the wider world)

As Freire pointed out, education can be either a tool of domestication or liberation so the choices we make in the organisation of groups inevitably reinforces or challenges oppression and discrimination.

However we organise groups, we have to recognise that for them to succeed learning has to take place. Carl Rogers (1990) said for people to learn there needs to be:

- real relationships underpinning the facilitation of learning;
- prizing, acceptance, trust;
- empathic understanding.

Learning in groups is mostly informal learning; members of the groups learn about each other, about the activities they are involved in, and about the wider world they interact with. Sometimes this learning involves the acquisition of existing knowledge from outside the group. At other times it involves the group creating its own new knowledge.

Alongside the development of knowledge is the development of skills and confidence. One of the purposes of group work is to provide mechanisms for collective support of group members to facilitate this learning.

It appears to be increasingly common for youth and community workers to recognise the learning needs of groups, but in the wrong way. Easy practice, or we could be more critical and call it lazy practice, is to offer groups formal training taken from a limited range of 'off-the-shelf courses'. This is of course an anathema for Freirean practice where the learning needs must be identified by the group participants themselves, through decoding generative themes. There are various ways in which more formal learning can be developed through groups and one of these methods is by Learning Circles (see Box 7.1).

BOX **7.1**

Learning Circles

Learning circles have been around for a long time in development work. They have developed from the simpler idea of a study group and are based on the principles and practices of effective adult learning. Learning circles can be defined as

> [s]mall, ongoing gatherings of people who come together to share their ideals, goals, practices and honest experiences in service learning. In all cases, learning circles seek to be free spaces where open discussion of hard questions can take place in a collaborative and enriching environment that brings together people from different constituencies.

(Purcell, 2005)

These circles are a flexible response to a variety of needs. Learning circles can be a distinct group in their own right or a smaller grouping within an organisation. Their function is to explore issues and ideas on behalf of themselves or the main group. The process and environment of learning circles are similar to traditional Freirean groups, the difference being that learning circles are less dependent upon the generative theme which is central to the Freirean approach, and more focused on immediate tasks and issues that need to be explored.

In contrast to delivering pre-planned short courses to groups, the open, supportive and participatory nature of learning circles facilitates participants to:

- *become more aware of their own thinking and reasoning;*
- *make their thinking and reasoning more visible to others;*
- *inquire into others' thinking and reasoning;*
- *inquire into what the observable facts are behind a statement;*
- *find out whether everyone agrees on what the facts are.*

Learning circles, however, only work when everyone is committed to the basic rules. Otherwise it's just another group setting. The key components of a learning circle are:

- *participate fully in the circle;*
- *communicate your needs;*
- *tell circle members and the facilitator whether or not your needs are being met;*
- *help members clarify their needs;*
- *respect their needs;*
- *help members exchange feedback, inquiry, and resources to meet their needs.*

The key to the success of a learning circle is the facilitator. It is essential to understand that the facilitation (as discussed elsewhere in this book) is not training in the traditional sense.

Stephen Brookfield (1991) has explored the factors that are essential for effective group work practice, and has identified six key principles which are congruent with Freirean practice.

1. Participation in learning is voluntary
Adults engage in learning as a result of their own volition. It may be that the circumstances prompting this learning are external to the learner (job loss, divorce, bereavement), but the decision to learn is the learner's own. Thus we can exclude those settings in which adults are coerced, bullied, or intimidated into learning.

2. Effective practice is characterised by a respect among participants for each other's self-worth
Educators must not engage in or seek to cultivate an environment in which behaviours, statements and practices take place that belittle or abuse others. This does not mean that criticism should be absent from educational encounters. It does mean that special attention has to be given to questions of self-worth.

3. Facilitation is collaborative
Facilitators and learners are engaged in a co-operative enterprise in which, at different times and for different purposes, leadership and facilitation roles will be assumed by different group members.

4. Praxis is placed at the heart of effective facilitation
Learners and facilitators are involved in a continual process of activity, collaborative analysis of activity, further reflection and collaborative analysis and so on.

5. Facilitation aims to foster in adults a spirit of critical reflection
Through educational encounters, learners come to appreciate that values, beliefs, behaviours and ideologies are culturally transmitted and that they are provisional and relative.

6. The aim of facilitation is the nurturing of self-directed, empowered adults
Such adults will see themselves as proactive, initiating individuals engaged in a continuous re-creation of their personal relationships, work worlds, and social circumstances rather than as reactive individuals, buffeted by uncontrollable forces of circumstance.

CASE STUDY

Community capacity building
It is generally recognised in the field that youth and community groups often need training support to maximise their potential. In one local authority staff were organised into Community Capacity Teams to deliver such training.

From a Freirean perspective the approach to this task would be to explore with groups a number of questions that focused on the overall objectives of the group, how the group operated and personal needs. For example:

• what they were trying to achieve;

• what skills and knowledge they needed to achieve this;

- *how well they felt the group was operating and what they required to improve this;*
- *what they needed personally.*

In order to really get to the essential needs it is necessary to go through a reflective process. People generally cannot answer these questions spontaneously. Once the group has worked through these questions bespoke courses or other learning experiences can be developed.

The Community Capacity Teams in common with much of local authority practice adopted a different approach. The workers devised a number of courses based around six meetings. The courses focused on a range of topics, including:

- *committee skills;*
- *chairing a meeting;*
- *health and safety;*
- *partnership policies and procedures;*
- *producing leaflets;*
- *first aid.*

The groups were then asked what they wanted from the list and the courses were duly delivered.

What is interesting here is the ideological contrast between the two approaches. The Community Capacity Teams decided what they thought the groups required. These courses were very functional. What is missing from their approach is anything that may relate to difficult questions around power, ideology, purpose and effectiveness of the work and relationships with the local authority. The courses on offer also fail to offer anything to help the group to work better or recognise individual needs.

The manner in which these courses were identified and delivered is also very disempowering. From knowing the workers involved, it is clear that they genuinely thought this would be empowering work and would meet people's needs.

The Tuckman model of group development

Bruce Tuckman (Tuckman and Jensen, 1977) developed a basic model of group development. He believed that group development falls into a series of distinctive stages (*forming – storming – norming – performing*) which are both necessary and inevitable. This is true for groups developed for Freirean purposes.

The Tuckman model is generally accepted, with various modifications, across a wide range of disciplines and activities. It has been used as a basis for the development of models of group dynamics, crucial to practice in social work group settings in outdoor education programmes, leadership development and experimental education, to name but a few.

Forming

In this phase group members are both testing out each other and the boundaries of group behaviour. We can only learn the norms of behaviour, and our individual position within the group, through this testing process. As this unfolds, group identity and the relative place of individuals within the group is created. Group leaders become identified (although this can change later) and dependency relationships begin to form.

Storming

As group development continues conflict and polarisation of attitudes can break out. Sometimes this is leadership conflict, at other times it is rebellion against the norms of the group. Questions about what the group is for, priorities and process are posed at this point.

Norming

Eventually the basic rules and order of the group are established and the conflicts of the storming phase resolved (this may or may not include people leaving the group). As the group norms are firmly established there will be a growth of feeling and cohesiveness, with new standards of behaviour being adopted and people becoming comfortable in group roles.

Performing

This is Tuckman's final stage, where all the structural issues of the group have been resolved. Group roles are increasingly functional and this allows them to be more flexibly applied. The members of the group are comfortable with their position and channel energy to collective activity. Everyone acts in a supportive way to enhance the possibility of group success.

Some writers believe there is a fifth stage, *mourning*. They argue that all groups have a life cycle, that ends with the group either successfully completing its task, failing to complete it, or just withering away.

In youth and community work how groups end is important. Many community activists will say that bad group experiences discourage people from entering into new group activity. It is therefore essential that the youth and community workers recognise when groups enter into their final stage, and either assist the group to end formally, or to be reborn as a new group. If this rebirth takes place the final stage therefore becomes one of *transforming* to a new set of activities, goals and membership.

There are far too many groups with the remnants of its membership talking about the good old days and lamenting the lack of interest in their current activities. It is understandable why people do this. Community-based groups can become the centre of an individual's social life. They may have taken people through emotional highs and lows, offered challenges, excitement and opportunities. It can therefore be difficult to recognise that this has gone, and to avoid the feeling of loss and grief people hold on. It is far better to organise an ending through a celebration of a group's life and its achievements.

ACTIVITY **7.2**

Think of a group in which you are an active member. Can you identify which of the Forming – Storming – Norming – Performing – Mourning/Transforming stages the group is currently in? Can you identify the previous stages of the group?

Secondly, think of a group you are facilitating. Do the Forming – Storming – Norming – Performing – Mourning/Transforming stages help you understand what is happening and what to do next?

It is useful to be able to understand the stage of development that groups are at since the role of the worker will vary from stage to stage. For example, the creative tension in the storming stage can help to establish the effectiveness of the group if the worker has the courage and skill to let it run.

Group work and development

Groups focused on youth and community work often generate a lot of practice and personal issues that need to be sympathetically and effectively addressed. One way of dealing with this is through the COMPASS model developed by Kelly and Sewell (see Figure 7.1).

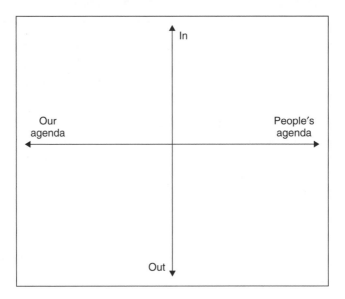

Figure 7.1 The COMPASS model

This simple model poses two basic questions for workers: whether we are inside or outside the process, and whether we are acting on our own or the group's agenda.

For the vertical axis (In or Out of the process), the essential question is about the relationship between the worker and the group. The majority of workers start as outsiders, even those who may live in the community. If their practice is based upon commitment, reliability, transparency and honesty they can become insiders. This is not always a good thing. Often workers need an external perspective and should not become over-identified with the group. This is a difficult balance as workers should balance being both an insider and outsider to the group. The COMPASS model provides a way for workers to identify their relative position with the group.

The horizontal axis (Our Agenda/People's Agenda) enables the worker to identify how far the group is being run for the benefit of an external agency or according to the expressed wishes of the group itself. This is a very difficult area as the worker will usually have a specific agency remit to carry through. Sometimes the group will also own this remit; sometimes they accept it by default. In Freirean practice the basic assumption is that the remit is owned by the group. Overall, classic Freirean group work would map to the top right-hand part of the model.

ACTIVITY **7.3**

Select a group where you are the worker. Map your approach to the group according to the COMPASS model.

- *Is this where you thought you would be?*

- *Is this where you want to be?*

- *What actions do you need to take with the group in the light of this activity?*

The individuals within the group often work through a range of personal and developmental issues. One way of understanding such changes is through the application of Johari's Window (named after its originators Joe Luft and Harry Ingham (1955)).

The table maps out areas that are known/unknown to you/others. The Free area maps knowledge that is known to you and other people; the Hidden area contains things about you that are known to you, but you wish to hide from other people. The Blind area contains things about you that other people know but you are unaware of. Finally the Mystery area contains information about you that is unknown.

	Known to Self	Not Known to Self
Known to Others	**FREE**	**BLIND**
Not Known to Others	**HIDDEN**	**MYSTERY**

Figure 7.2 Johari's Window

ACTIVITY **7.4**

Complete Johari's Window for yourself relative to a group of friends. What personal attributes would you put in the Free and Hidden boxes? Ask your friends what they would put in the Free and Blind boxes.

One of the key purposes of youth and community work and Freirean practice is to assist individuals to enlarge the Free area, to become less Blind about themselves and be confident enough to reduce the Hidden area. Although the Mystery area may be reduced, it will always be there, as we can never truly know ourselves. Thoughtful readers will see the link between this activity and Freire's concern with boundary issues and the increased self-awareness from engaging in a process of critical consciousness.

As well as the personal development concerns, group work for youth and community workers is concerned with changing the world to some degree. There need to be clear developmental tasks which lead to defined outcomes. This style of group work can be summarised in Figure 7.3 (Drysdale and Purcell, 1999, p81). The task for the worker is to simultaneously (although the relative emphasis on the three components will vary over time) balance the group process with individual development and group tasks.

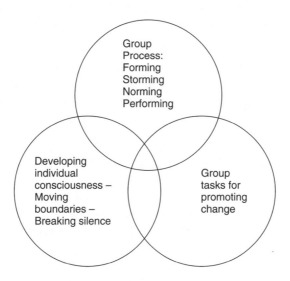

Figure 7.3

Understanding power relationships

Implicit within human activity is the deployment of power. By this we mean the *motivation and capacity to act, to make changes and to influence the actions of others*. Power itself is neither a good or bad thing, it is what power is used for that can be the problem.

Foucault pointed out that power is essentially the application of knowledge. In the UK we are seldom, if ever, physically forced to do something. We voluntarily limit or modify our actions because we believe this to be the right, accepted, or inevitable thing to do. The reader will remember that this has been discussed during our exploration of hegemony and its manifestation through boundary situations.

Many youth and community workers believe that they do not have power and that they are at the service of the community. This is not so. Workers have power, simply by being a worker and a representative of an agency. Sometimes this means that workers, in carrying out the demands of their employing agency, act to reinforce hegemony. In addition workers have personal power in that they usually have knowledge, skills and experience that group members do not have. This is as it should be – otherwise why are the workers there? This is not to ignore or undervalue the fact that group members will bring their knowledge and skills to the group.

In terms of group work it is important to explore who holds power within the group. This can be formal power (the group chair) or informal power (the person who speaks most and/or commands most respect within the group). This can often be the worker, even though they may claim to be powerless.

Groups with an external agenda also need to map where power lies in their areas of interest. Is it with councillors or local officials? Often the appearance of power is not the same thing as actual power. The local mayor may appear to be very powerful when senior council officials actually make the key decisions.

One of the key purposes for Freirean work is to change the power relationships in a local area. This can be achieved in a number of ways; through mobilising people, building organisations, using the media, or organising events. Sometimes it comes from local groups exploring issues and creating new knowledge that contests current belief around what is correct and appropriate activity. At other times it can be brought about by enabling new community leaders to develop and emerge.

Youth and community workers need to recognise that community leaders usually have limited power bases; often their influence extends only over a few people or single issues. Often this is ignored and community leaders, for the convenience of agencies, are described as having wide influence over the community in general. This is seldom the case. Sometimes the existing community leadership is part of the local problem.

Workers need to analyse power relationships, and there are basic tools that enable this:

- the *positional method* analyses who holds power in formal organisations;
- the *reputational method* looks at who holds power in informal settings;
- the *decisional method* is based upon analysing who actually makes the key decisions;
- the *social participation method* maps who holds power in the community based on networks of relationships.

ACTIVITY 7.5

Select an established group you know well.

- *Who are the leaders within this group?*
- *What is their leadership position based upon?*
- *Does the exercise of this leadership enhance or inhibit the activities of the group?*

ACTIVITY 7.6

Select a community-based group and analyse the different power relationships using the positional, reputational, decisional, and social participation methods in turn.

- *What do these four sets of analyses tell you?*
- *What are the implications for the group from this analysis?*

The danger is that, when supporting groups, workers can be too focused on tasks rather than focusing on the group and their process. Group work theory provides a framework that gives due attention to both process and product.

C H A P T E R   R E V I E W

In this chapter we have looked at the different nature of community-based groups, and the various ways in which they can be run. We have explored Tuckman's model of group development and Brookfield's views on the underlying approach to progressive and enabling group work. We have discussed the relationship between the worker and the group, personal development within the group and the change focus of community based groups. Finally, we have addressed the basic issues of power relationships both within groups and their relationships to wider structures.

FURTHER READING

Drysdale, J and Purcell, R (1999) Breaking the culture of silence: Group work and community development. *Group Work,* 11(3): 70–87.

This article explores the relationship between group work and the wider development process.

Tuckman, BW and Jensen, MAC (1977) Stages of small group development revisited. *Group and Organizational Studies,* 2: 419–427.

This is the classic article exploring the idealised stages of group development.

Chapter 8

Developing generative themes for community action

CHAPTER OBJECTIVES

This chapter looks at some basic ideas around participation. We then discuss the implications for the worker's role, problem posing and the importance of promoting dialogue. The chapter then explores what is meant by 'generative themes' and how they can be developed through the use of listening surveys.

This chapter provides underpinning knowledge for workers to think about and develop their practice in the following key Community Development Occupational areas (PAULO, 2003):

- Key Role A: Develop relationships with communities and organisations;

- Key Role B: Encourage people to work with and learn from each other;

- Key Role C: Work with people in communities to plan for change and take collective action.

It also addresses these Key Youth Work Standards (LLUK, 2008):

- 1.1.5 Support young people in taking action and to tackle problems;

- 1.4.2 Enable young people to access information and to make decisions;

- 4.2.3 Identify and address new youth work opportunities.

Why have participative methods?

The main rationale for participative methods is based on the belief that people themselves are best placed to know what their problems are and, with the right support, can develop the most appropriate solutions to those problems. It is therefore incumbent on workers to develop approaches which tap into that local knowledge and capacity for change. To do anything else is to impose external culture and values and, even for the best of reasons, further disempower the communities we work with. As Paulo Freire puts it:

One cannot expect positive results from an educational or political action program which fails to respect the particular view of the world held by the people. Such a program constitutes cultural invasion, good intentions notwithstanding.

(Freire, 1972, p93)

There is no such thing as a neutral position, and it has to be recognised that youth and community work is about taking sides. The National Occupational Standards for

Community Development Work recognise this and identify promoting social justice as a core value underpinning practice. As the great American community organiser Saul Alinsky commented, this means taking the side of the have-nots, those who are left out and over-looked (1989). Workers therefore have to be on their guard for policies and initiatives which, although purporting to be for community empowerment, actually impose the vision, values and agenda of outside bodies.

The current social policy context in the UK has much to say about participation but as the classic analysis by Shelly Arnstein (1969) reveals, not everything which claims to be partici-pative gives local people a genuine say in the issues that affect their lives. Often what is described by professionals as participation is simply information giving, or a consultation exercise where the community is presented with a limited range of pre-determined options. Even where partnership structures are established there are usually significant power and resource imbalances between the community and agencies. Genuine examples of participation where the community has equality with agencies are rare.

Aspects of social justice and participation (from the National Occupational Standards for Community Development Work)

Social justice

- *Respecting and valuing diversity and difference;*
- *Challenging oppressive and discriminatory actions and attitudes;*
- *Addressing power imbalances between individuals, within groups and society;*
- *Committing to pursue civil and human rights for all;*
- *Seeking and promoting policy and practices that are just and enhance equality whilst challenging those that are not.*

Participation

- *Promoting the participation of individuals and communities, particularly those tradition-ally marginalised/excluded;*
- *Recognising and challenging barriers to full and effective participation;*
- *Supporting communities to gain skills to engage in participation;*
- *Developing structures that enable communities to participate effectively;*
- *Sharing good practice in order to learn from each other.*

It would be fair to say that youth and community workers often find themselves in the sit-uation where they are trying to develop local participation in issues, services and events which have been decided outside the community. This could range from trying to get people to use the new 'one-stop shop', to getting participants for pre-decided training courses, to persuading people to engage in local authority-led community planning processes.

There are several implications which flow from this model of practice. Firstly, the fundamental power relationships within the community have not changed; external bodies are still making decisions on behalf of local people, albeit with some marginal choices being left to them. Secondly, the worker has to supply large amounts of time and emotional energy trying to persuade people that these are issues and services which are important to them. This can lead to workers burning out and communities feeling as if they are being battered by regular waves of new policies and initiatives and becoming even more 'apathetic' and 'hard to reach'. This calls into question the sustainability of this model, both for workers and communities. Finally, if all of this energy and effort is going into working with issues that are not necessarily the community's main concern it means that our practice masks these real concerns and further silences and disempowers the community.

An alternative form of practice must therefore be employed. In the rest of this chapter we suggest that workers need, as their first point of departure, to help communities focus on the issues which are of concern to them and, importantly, which they are prepared and able to do something about. Let us then consider the role of the worker in this alternative model of practice.

What is the worker's role?

Since the 1960s most youth and community workers have come to believe that their role is not that of the expert who decides what is best, but to help people themselves decide what their needs are and how best to meet them (Batten, 1967). However the role is multi-faceted, complex and contested by different theorists and stakeholders in the field of community development.

In the current social policy context in the UK workers find themselves caught between conflicting role demands. Indeed, this has always been so. On one hand the principles and

---

Youth work and community work
The National Occupational Standards for Youth Work defines the key purpose of youth work as being to:

> [e]nable young people to develop holistically, working with them to facilitate their personal, social and educational development, to enable them to develop their voice, influence and place in society and to reach their full potential.

The National Occupational Standards for Community Work identifies the key purpose of community development work as to work collectively to bring about social change and justice, by working with communities to:

- identify their needs, opportunities, rights and responsibilities;

- plan, organise and take action;

- evaluate the effectiveness and impact of the action.

. . . all in ways which challenge oppression and tackle inequalities.

values of community development casts workers in the role of developing people's ability to think critically and act to effect authentic, sustainable social change. On the other there are expectations for them to be deliverers of services with prescribed targets and outputs to be met. Workers will have to negotiate and sometimes fight to have a space to practice under the first set of expectations in order to make a difference in the communities which they serve. As Peter McLaren puts it: *We require a revolutionary movement of educators informed by a principled ethics of compassion and social justice, a social ethos based on solidarity and social interdependence* (1998, p451).

Unlike the work of Batten, whose response to the challenge of enabling people to take control of their own lives is that of non-direction, theorists such as Freire, McLaren and Ledwith suggest an approach to practice which is underpinned by particular concerns and commitments. Ledwith (2005) identifies five vital areas: a commitment to collective action for social and environmental justice; a process of empowerment through critical consciousness and participation; an analysis of power and discrimination; an understanding of the dominant ideas and the wider political context; and collective action based on this analysis which deals with root causes and not just symptoms. It is clear from this that the worker is not a blank canvas who, with no previous experience or values, seeks only to work with the community's agenda. Rather they are intentionally agents of change seeking to encourage sustainable social change through critical reflection and collective action.

This is particularly important here at the early part of the twenty-first century, because the current dominant ideology that shapes social policy and practice is that of the individual. Explanations of social problems centre increasingly around individual pathology or family inadequacies. Putnam's work (2001) also alerts us to the erosion of social capital in our postmodern world. The disintegration of networks of formal relationships – trade unions, churches, clubs and organisations – and the nuclearisation of the family have meant that people increasingly face social problems on their own. In addition to this we understand from the work of Gramsci (1971) that the process of hegemony embeds the values and identity of the ruling class in the minds of those who are ruled. This renders the experience of people in marginalised communities as normal and inevitable and unchangeable. It also casts the response to social issues in the terms of the current dominant discourse. Therefore issues of youth unemployment might be understood in terms of lack of appropriate parenting and not in the context of wider societal and structural issues.

It becomes clear then that approaches to empowerment of communities in which workers simply go and ask people what they want are surely doomed to failure since, without a process of critical reflection, people will inevitably respond to symptoms rather than root causes and even the symptoms will be understood and responded to in the light of the dominant discourse of individual pathology.

And so the role of the worker in a model of practice which leads to genuine empowerment is this. Firstly, to have a thorough understanding of the issues which are important to the local community. Secondly, to understand the wider social and political context that gives rise to those local conditions. Thirdly, to develop processes whereby local people can critically reflect on their experiences in the context of the wider world. And finally, to support a process of collective action that aims to achieve personal and social transformation.

ACTIVITY 8.1

Think of a group situation that you have been involved with recently.

- *Who officially had power in this setting?*
- *Who else might have executed power through personality, relationships, etc.?*
- *How did that affect the functioning of the group?*
- *What messages were implicit in this about gender, class, ethnicity, etc.?*

Assume that you are working with this group.

- *How might you promote personal and social transformation?*
- *What power does the worker bring to this situation?*
- *What are the range of effects this could have on the group?*
- *How do you ethically justify intervening in this way?*

Problem-posing methods

As we have established, the first step in the process of a transformational practice is helping people to question the social reality in which they live, with all its injustices and contradictions, but which they experience as normality. Ira Shor (1993, p26) describes this as a process of questioning answers rather than merely answering questions. Through this process people cease to be objects and become writers of their own story (Jesson and Newman, 2004).

Within this model of practice workers develop materials and process which enable people to critically reflect on their social and material conditions and analyse them in the context of the wider world. This suggests a democratisation of learning since the knowledge which is created and the conclusion which is drawn are not within the gift of the worker but are created by the group. It also indicates a shifting of power from the individual expert to the group. Not that this is an easy or automatic process – far from it. Because of the unequal social relations we all live in, we automatically default to our socially conditioned roles. It is therefore very common for workers to feel that they must have all the answers and for the groups they are working with to defer to their expertise and look for direction and answers. These ingrained social roles must be struggled against if real empowerment is to be achieved.

Problem-posing methods use codifications of generative themes as their starting point. Essentially, these are concrete representations of an aspect of people's lived reality. For example a group could be presented with photographs of housing conditions on their estate. This has the effect of enabling them to see again images that have become invisible to them. It is at this stage that the problem-posing method starts.

A typical range of questions that the group might explore are:

- What do you see happening?

- Why is it happening this way?

- How do people feel in this situation?

- Whose interest does it serve?

- Who holds power in this situation?

- Is your experience the same or different to this?

- Are there any things happening economically or politically which are having an impact on this situation?

- Is there anything being done to improve this situation?

- Is there anything we could do to improve it?

- How might we do this?

- Who else could be involved?

The result of these discussions will be a critical understanding of the issue, personal awareness of the individual's relationship to the issue, understanding that the issue is experienced collectively, and an outline for a programme of action. The role of the worker is to facilitate this process, to learn from it, but not to direct it. Inevitably this often raises issues for the worker when the programme of action may conflict with agency agendas.

Dialogue

Inherent in the worker's role to facilitate discussion is an understanding of the idea of dialogue. Freire describes dialogue as a form of revolutionary communication (Freire, 1972). From this we can see that he is describing not a mere conversation but communication set in a context of two transformed relationships; this is an intentional process. Although it is not prescriptive in its outcomes it is trying to achieve something in particular and that is *conscientisation*. This is a state which Freire describes as

> *[a] particular quality of critical awareness which enables people to consider a range of options in the ways they act, and enables them to choose a course of action deliberately and with the intention to change some aspect of their reality.*

> (1972, p101)

It is built on two sets of transformed relationships: the relationship between teachers and learners, and the relationship between learners and knowledge.

> *Educator and learners all become learners assuming the same attitude as cognitive subjects discovering knowledge through one another and through the objects they try to know. It is not a situation where one knows and the others do not; it is rather a search, by all, at the same time to discover something by the act of knowing which cannot exhaust all the possibilities in the relation between object and subject.*

> (Freire, 1976, p115)

In order to achieve this transformation, the worker must understand the culture and community which is the social location of the learner and then cross the border. In that way they act in solidarity with the learners; no longer seeing them as *the other* (Mayo, 1999). The starting point for this learning process is that no one knows the full picture, neither the teacher nor the learner, but that together we can discover new knowledge. This does not mean that the worker has the same role as the learner but that they have complementary roles in the group as the whole group both teaches and learns.

As an example, a youth worker might want to discuss sexual health with a group of young people. In a traditional form of practice what was to be learned would be decided by the worker; this could be the use of condoms, the nature of sexual diseases, and/or available health resources. The worker might then set up group discussions, screen videos, distribute leaflets and arrange visits to other projects in order to enable the group to learn what the worker had decided were the important lessons for the group. We can see that in this model, the worker does not learn but only teaches, and the group learns. No matter how well meaning, this is external knowledge imposed on the group from outside. For people to act on knowledge they must believe in it, and this is unlikely to happen when it is simply the case of adults once again telling them what is right and wrong. Perhaps this is one of the reasons why sexual health amongst young people in the UK is so bad.

By contrast a transformational approach to the subject of sexual health would be qualitatively different. The worker, realising she does not know all there is to know about the sexual health issues that are important to the group, would seek to know what young people understand, experience and feel about sexual health issues, as well as understanding the received wisdom about safe sex practices. These elements would then be explored by the group through dialogue. Within this understandings and assumptions would be challenged in order to develop authentic understanding of how people are positioned within the issue. The outcome of the dialogue would not be known since it is developed by the group and not the worker. They might think that issues of identity and power are more central to them in making positive decisions about their sexual behaviour. This might also include much of the information contained in the traditional approach but the young people themselves would decide what was useful and how it fitted into their own understanding of the world. In this way an internal impetus for change is developed rather than the external imposition of the traditional approach.

From this we can see that within traditional forms of practice, knowledge is seen as an approved commodity which must be successfully transmitted from teaches to learners; knowledge is not changed. To paraphrase Foucault, *knowledge is power*, and youth and community workers need to recognise this fundamental point. Within transformative education, existing knowledge is the starting point and is to be critically examined through co-investigation of the learning group. Through this process of co-investigation new understandings are developed and new knowledge is created. Because this knowledge is created and owned by the group it has power.

Part of the effectiveness of this social approach to learning is its ability to enable us to analyse our assumptions – why we think the things we think. This can reveal the boundaries which block us from developing new ideas and new action.

What is a generative theme?

In order to galvanise community action, the worker must first identify issues about which people have a passion and a willingness to take some action. Freire calls these issues generative themes. He identifies domination and liberation as the overarching or global generative themes. These global themes are expressed at every level within society. People experience them as boundary situations. An example of a boundary situation from community-based education is the very common experience of working with a group of community activists who, although intelligent and able, feel stupid and non-educable. This understanding of themselves could have been produced by things teachers have said to them, failing in formal education and believing when they are told by other members of the community that education is not for them. However it is produced, it feels like a real and insurmountable barrier which will effectively keep them from risking education; which further strengthens the barrier. Only when they begin to see an alternative future for themselves and are able to see the injustice of the education system that failed them and a society which is prepared to put them on the scrapheap – and get angry about it – do they have the ability to challenge that barrier.

And so, a generative theme is an issue about which people feel strongly and are willing to take some action about. Much of the government-sponsored youth and community work we see today flows out of centrally determined strategies by which local issues and projects are identified. This results in workers spending much of their time recruiting local people into programmes that they did not choose. This is not only inefficient but it casts workers as subjects and the community as objects to be worked on thereby strengthening feelings of alienation and disempowerment. Freire describes a transformative relationship between workers and the people.

> To investigate the generative theme is to investigate people's thinking about reality and people's action upon reality, which is their praxis. For precisely this reason, the methodology proposed requires that the investigators and the people (who would normally be considered objects of that investigation) should act as co-investigators. The more active an attitude men and women take in regard to the exploration of their thematics, the more they deepen their critical awareness of reality and, in spelling out those thematics, take possession of that reality.

(Freire, 1972, p78)

However, a generative theme is not something that comes automatically; it has to be worked for. This is in part because our education system does not invite us to be critical thinkers, leading us to passively accept the situations we find ourselves in. Freire describes this as a state of Magical Consciousness typified by fatalism, disempowerment and passivity (Ledwith, 2005) where people feel powerless to change. People also come to take for granted the conditions they live in; these become both inevitable and invisible to them. On one occasion I was talking to a young man who lived in a run-down area of Glasgow. When I asked him if he had ever experienced any discrimination in his life he said no. This was despite the fact that he had been unemployed for several years, had addiction problems and was living in poor-standard housing in a state of long-term poverty. It was several days into the programme we were going through that he came back to me in amazement. 'I've been discriminated against all my life!' he said, but up to that point he hadn't been able to see it and could not therefore take any steps to change.

It is also difficult because encounters between workers and the people they work with are encounters of power. The workers, whether they want it or not, have status, experience, and access to resources. The community have learned to be dependent, reliant on author-ity figures and passive. An essential element in the process of individual and social transformation is the struggle to transform this worker/client – teacher/learner relation-ship. Through dialogue, which we discuss in detail below, people find voice and value which can enable, even briefly, these contradictions to be transcended. It is this experience that begins to build a vision of a more human, more democratic, more nurturing and cre-ative world.

Often communities are described as apathetic but their education and experience has taught and conditioned them to be passive and silent. The worker must therefore find cre-ative ways to enable people to re-see their lives and to examine their assumptions, what they have taken for granted about it. This examination is often a disturbing and emotional process leaving people feeling angry that they have endured the situation for so long. This emotional energy is an indispensable aspect of a transformational process; it is the fuel that initiates and sustains action. If the issue you are working on does not engender emo-tion and passion, it is not a generative theme; any action that flows from it is likely to fizzle out or require the worker to cajole people along.

Listening surveys

Traditional forms of practice usually rely on qualitative and quantitative research methods to provide an evidence base for practice. The inherent danger in these approaches is that inevitably the worker's own experience and value-base will shape the issues focused on, and the questions asked will in turn shape the answers obtained and the action that results. For example an organisation which has been set up to deliver skills training to get people back into work may well carry out some initial research to identify what the com-munity wants. It will of course ask training-related questions and get training-related answers. This will then justify the action they take within the community as being 'community-led'. It is obvious that if you asked the same group of people different ques-tions, you would get a very different picture of what the community needed.

Often these studies treat local communities and the people within them as data sets to be analysed. Needs are usually ascribed according to agency priorities rather than the openly expressed views of local people. The overall effect is to treat people as objects for analysis and organisation, rather than subjects who have the right to self-determination. The Freirean approach seeks to reverse these power relationships and support local people to define both the needs of the area in which they live and the solution to their problems. Key to this process is the creation of generative themes. An example of a generative theme is shown in Table 8.1.

One practical way of identifying a generative theme within a community is by carrying out a listening survey. Listening in this context denotes a permanent attitude on the part of

Table 8.1 Generative themes

Theme	Economic causes of the problem	Who controls the decision-making on the problem?	What are the culture, values and beliefs held about the problem?	What is the present national, provincial, and/or local policy on the problem?
Young people drinking on street corners	Limited disposable income; Access to cheap drink; Lack of job prospects; Few youth venues	Parents; Shop owners; Police; Local authority	Drinking is a sign of being grown up; Need to drink to be accepted by peer group	WHO Declaration on Young People and Alcohol, 2001; Crime & Disorder Act 1998; Parenting Orders; Confiscation of Alcohol (Young Persons) Act 1997

the subject who is listening, of being open to the word of the other, to the gesture of the other, to the differences of the other (Freire, 1998, p107). The key skill in a listening survey is having an open mind. As Purcell commented:

For this (listening survey) to work it is important to adopt the Zen approach of expecting nothing. That is to be open to anything and any interpretation and not to approach with a mind fixed on particular sets of issues or an attachment to a specific course of action.

(Purcell, 2005, p239)

A listening survey can be a challenging task as people's feelings may be contradictory and are seldom clearly expressed. Often a 'presenting issue' such as young people on the streets may be a symptom which hides the underlying issues (for example the lack of youth provision and difficult home environments).

Hope and Timmel (1999) outline the nature of a listening survey. Teams of workers, often made up of a mixture of development workers and local people, seek to identify the issues within the community that people have the strongest feelings about. The process is to find situations where people are involved in informal conversations – shops, bars, outside schools, waiting rooms, etc. – and listen for the issues about which people are worried, happy, sad, angry or fearful. In particular the team is listening for issues which relate to six themes which are common to groups of people living together:

1 meeting basic physical needs;

2 relationships between people;

3 community decision-making processes and structures;

4 education and socialisation;

5 recreation and beliefs;

6 values.

The key issues are then presented back to the community by the use of codes – discussed in detail in the next chapter – which lead to critical reflection and collective action.

ACTIVITY 8.2

Ask someone to tell you in detail (for ten minutes) about their family.

- *Respond with a summary of what you have heard.*
- *Pick out the three most important things that they said.*
- *Make one recommendation.*
- *Discuss the accuracy and usefulness of your observation.*

This exercise highlights both the need for accurate listening and the need to check your understanding with the people you are working with.

ACTIVITY 8.3

With another person, visit somewhere where people congregate – a café, pub, bus stop, or a school gate. At this stage you must work separately.

- *Listen out for issues that people are concerned, happy or angry about.*
- *Summarise the issues.*
- *Make one suggestion for action.*

Then compare your findings with those of the other person and discuss similarities and differences.

C H A P T E R   R E V I E W

Workers must seek out generative themes within communities in order to harness the energy and passion to achieve social change. Genuine participation will come about through engaging people in the critical examination of their lives and providing structures to support action on the themes that emerge. This approach to working with people seeks to support empowerment that leads to genuine change. As such it acts as an antidote and stands as a critique of top-down approaches which seek only to ameliorate symptoms and pacify people.

FURTHER READING

Hope, A and Timmel, S (1999) *Training for Transformation Vols 1–4.* London: ITDG Publishing.

This is in many ways the classic text of popular education practice. It provides a wide range of ways to both think about and practice popular education in ways which are accessible to youth and community groups. There are a variety of exercises which are spelled out in detail; as with all material the worker should adapt it to suit the needs of their particular group.

Chapter 9

Using codes: Critical reflection for practice

CHAPTER OBJECTIVES

This chapter presents a range of contexts within which codes can be usefully employed. A code here is defined as a concrete representation of people's lived experience which is used in the context of dialogue in order to engage people in critical reflection and action in order to effect social change. They are not just the use of visual aids to get a discussion going. They are the product of identifying a generative theme and carefully devising an image, a song, a play, a piece of text or other experience which will allow the group to fully explore and act on that theme.

Listening surveys and codes

As previously discussed, this is a method of getting to the issues that are really important to people within the community; it is a way of circumventing the pet issues of policymakers, agencies and workers and actually working to the community's agenda. The basic idea is for the worker to find out what people love, hate, are passionate about, fear, and so on – these are the issues which people will organise around.

ACTIVITY 9.1

List the types of things within a community you know well that people would feel strongly enough about to do something about. Are they the same issues that local agencies are working on?

The survey can be carried out by asking very open-ended questions and listening to the answers of the respondents and drawing the generative themes from that or by simply listening in on people's unstructured conversations in a variety of public places and drawing the generative themes from that. In either case these themes form the basis for the process of codification, de-codification and action which is at the heart of popular education. It is therefore well worth spending some time on this stage to ensure that you have hit on the right theme.

At this stage a worker's creativity is brought to the fore – how is it possible to make a concrete representation of this abstract theme in a way which will allow people to see the issue in a fresh way, critically examine it and prepare for and take action? This is no mechanistic exercise; this is community development as an art form.

Let's take the example of community safety. Through your careful listening to the community you may have identified that there are levels of fear within the community which are limiting people's ability to make choices and take action. There are a variety of ways in which you could codify that issue. You could devise role plays in which people could experience their threats or perceived threats from the point of view of different characters. You could use a song which deals with aspects of the issue. Or you could develop a range of photographic images to make the issue visible. In any event the key is found by getting the issue right and using a code which communicates with the group. Clearly a code that will work with a group of young people might not work with an elderly group.

ACTIVITY 9.2

Imagine you have been asked to work on the issues of sexual health with a group of young people. Devise a code that would allow the group to explore the issue and come up with their own responses, rather than having answers imposed on them.

What are the ethical issues involved in this activity and how would you deal with them?

CASE STUDY

Participative research and codes

Photovoice is a method of using photography to develop codes to critically examine people's lived conditions which result in collective action. An example of this is the work documented by Wang et al. (2004) in Flint, Michigan. They describe Photovoice as participatory-action research methodology based on the understanding that people are experts on their own lives. Using the Photovoice methodology, participants allow their photographs to raise the questions, 'Why does this situation exist? Do we want to change it, and, if so, how?'

In this situation they worked with 40 people from their neighbourhood and professional photographers to document the impact of violence on community life. An example of what was produced was an iconic photograph entitled 'Exploded Frustration' taken by Eric Dutro, a 17-year-old participant, which featured a bullet-hole on his bus. Eric wrote, 'I can tell that the bus I ride in is always different because the bullet holes are always in different windows.' These images and text then became the object of the group's reflection. These reflections happened around the mnemonic 'SHOWeD':

- S – What do we SEE or how do we name this problem?
- H – What is really HAPPENING?
- O – How does this story relate to OUR lives?
- W – WHY does this problem or strength exist? What are the root causes?
- E – How might we become EMPOWERED now that we better understand the problem?
- D – What can we DO about it?

From these dialogues community themes emerged; they defined a 'theme' as having at least four compelling photographs and stories that emerged during group discussion. These themes were then presented to policy-makers and community leaders and have impacted on public policy and levels of community engagement within that neighbourhood.

Planning

Ideal Community

This exercise can be used when thinking of the community as a whole or about particular aspects or projects. The idea is to use visual methods rather than words and text to explore people's visions and goals. This often has the effect of helping people to step outside their conventional ideas and discover new ways of thinking about the issue.

Method

Using images from magazines and newspapers the group is invited to build their ideal community. This works best in small groups of three or four people. People are encouraged to be creative and experimental; there are no wrong answers at this stage.

If there is more than one group, they can share their images with each other, leading to dialogue and perhaps the development of images which express the whole group's vision and goals for the issue.

This then becomes the focus of the group's critical examination, perhaps using the kind of questions discussed in Chapter 6:

- What do you see happening?
- Why is it happening this way?
- How do people feel in this situation?
- Whose interest does it serve?
- Who holds power in this situation?
- Is your experience the same or different to this?
- Are there any things happening economically or politically which are having an impact on this situation?
- Is there anything being done to improve this situation?
- Is there anything we could do to improve it?
- How might we do this?
- Who else could be involved?

Outcome

This whole process gives people the opportunity to think deeply about the issue and the wider social, political and economic context which it occupies. It will also generate options for action, suggest tactics and alliances and focus on priorities.

Future basing

This is a tool used within the world of business which can be adapted as a participative and empowering way of planning action or reshaping organisations.

Method

Ask the group to picture themselves five years in the future and imagine that their project has been very successful. Ask them then to think of specific things that would exist within the project; these could include resources, activities, processes or people. Participants then write down these things on sticky notes and the worker themes the responses. The group then use these themed responses as their code and analyse them in terms of the questions posed above.

Alternatively participants could draw their responses. These could then be used as the basis of a map which could outline destinations, milestones, hazards and roadblocks.

Outcome

This technique clarifies the group's mission by exploring alternatives and agreeing on a common destination. The use of text or images forces people to be more specific about their plans and allows differences of perception to be explored and consensus to be built.

It also allows groups to prioritise and timetable action and to take stock of and plan for difficulties which will be encountered as they take action. This record or image can then form the basis of monitoring and evaluating the progress of the group towards their goals and alert them to the need for change in direction or tactics.

Group processes

Group identity

How people see themselves and are seen by others has a powerful effect on how they feel, how they act and what opportunities are open to them. The two examples below show how a group can both analyse and celebrate who they are.

Method 1

Discuss with the group their favourite song or the first CD they bought and explore why it is important to them and what images and feelings it evokes.

You could then listen to other forms of music, including national and other anthems (football, political, etc.) and discuss how they affect us.

Using simple musical forms develop an anthem for the group – something that expresses who they are and what they bring to the world.

This code is now examined by the group.

Outcome

Because music deals with deeper emotional issues, this approach gets beyond the mere facts and touches how people feel. The worker should not underestimate the power of this type of work and should build in time to pick up the emotional fallout that it can produce.

It allows people to examine the assumptions they have about themselves and that other people have about them and how this can limit the choices they have. By being able to develop new ways of expressing who they are, they begin to think of themselves differently; and feel differently. This perceptual and emotional shift can help to fuel subsequent individual and collective action for change.

Method 2

The use of banners to define and celebrate a group's identity has a long tradition through trade unions, the women's movement and other campaigning organisations. In the context of popular education this process can be something which enables people to examine and challenge their own and others' perceptions of them as a springboard for positive action for change.

Banners can be created using a wide range of techniques. It can be useful to work alongside artists and crafts people if the banner is to be permanent in nature. However it is created, the intention is the same – creating a series of images and text which capture the essence of what the group want to say about themselves to the wider world.

As a starting point for this you might want to explore what other people say about the group through the media and sharing personal stories. This will reveal both the positives and negatives and will allow the group to explore why those images exist and what impact they have on them and their life opportunities. From this people may have a sense that they want to put the record straight by celebrating who they really are and the strengths that they have as a group.

Outcome

Both the process and the outcome provide a strengthening of the group's identity. This can be particularly important if the group feels that they are under siege or misrepresented and want to reclaim their identity. This strong collective image can help to strengthen the commitment to collective action and having a collective voice.

Unsticking a group

The power of using codes with a group that is stuck – i.e. which is experiencing tensions and have lost sight of their purpose – is that, where discussions often lead to polarisation and defensiveness, the use of images to mediate between people seems to set a better context for useful dialogue and resolution.

Method

Ask each member of the group to create an image that expresses how they feel about the group at the present time. Each member then shares their image with the whole group which results in dialogue around people's experiences and feelings about the group. A further representation can then be made which represents the group's common themes, the obstacles they are facing and strategies to overcome them.

Outcome

This way of working provides a safe environment for people to explore their feelings and feel heard in a difficult situation. From a place of openness and honesty, the group can then refocus on the issues which unite them and have a collective strength to move forward.

C H A P T E R   R E V I E W

The use of codes and what can be used as codes is limited only by the imagination of the worker. The strength of the code is that it accesses people's visual and creative resources and utilises these to think deeply and solve problems. They are risky of course because the worker has no control over the end point – groups actually do take control over their own destinies, even if it is only for a short time. It is however this experience of taking power that provides the motivation to continue the process of asking questions, making demands and not settling for the way things are at present. Codes provide an emotional, enjoyable way of becoming active in your own life and the life of your community.

FURTHER READING

Sheehy, M and Warner, C (2001) *Partners Companion Manual to Training for Transformation*. Dublin: Partners.

This is a compilation of the exercises, processes and methods designed and used by facilitators over several years and drawing on experience of workshops in the north and south of Ireland, the UK and across the world.

Chapter 10
Participation

CHAPTER OBJECTIVES

In the Youth Work and Community Development Work National Occupational Standards, participation is an underpinning value and implicit across all of the standards. But what do we mean by participation, how should it inform the practice of youth and community workers and how does this fit with Freirean practice?

This chapter explores these questions. We then look at examples of how the ideals of participation can be applied to youth and community work practice at both a micro- and a macro-level.

Contested ideas of participation

Some writers see participation as a collective mass activity at grass roots level, and this would include those coming from a Freirean or a PRA (Participative Rapid Appraisal) perspective. Some radical commentators suggest that the idea of participation simply promotes a myth of classlessness and equality of power (see for example Coit, 1978). Other writers believe that participation is best achieved through selecting community 'representatives' to act on behalf of the wider community. This latter position is the mainstream view of practice within the UK.

All these positions are problematic. Mass activity can only operate meaningfully at a small scale. Community representatives are seldom representative of anything other than a small constituency. The radical discourse often leads to collective disengagement from the process of change.

ACTIVITY 10.1

Michel Foucault said that power comes from discourse. By this he means that, if all we talk about is participation and partnerships, they then become the new orthodoxy, and alternative ways of working begin to be seen as strange, out of date, unfashionable, or unacceptable. In effect the world changes because the way we talk about it changes.

Discuss with colleagues who influences this discussion in the community where you work.

Paul Brickell (2000), commenting on the drive to increase community participation in the UK, argues that over the past 20 years or so a consultation industry has developed within the public services. The effect of this drive towards consultation has diverted local people's energy away from direct creative and useful work in their communities, to sitting on committees and boards to fulfil the agenda of local government. Also referring to UK practice, Marjory Mayo argues (1997) that if such community involvement is to move beyond the tokenistic there needs to be increased and open flows of information, independent advice, proactiveness by the community organisations, and control over resources, leading to more direct community control on implementation. The point that Mayo made in 1997 is still true today.

The classic text on participation comes from Shelly Arnstein (1969), writing about practice in the USA. Arnstein understood very well that participation, like all community-based activity, has ideological underpinnings and could be used to manipulate local communities just as easily as for power sharing or progressive change. For her the purpose of participation is:

> the redistribution of power that enables the have-not citizens, presently excluded from the political and economic processes, to be deliberately included in the future. It is the strategy by which the have-nots join in determining how information is shared, goals and policies are set, tax resources are allocated, programmes are operated, and benefits like contracts and patronage are parcelled out. In short it is the means by which they can induce significant reform which enables them to share in the benefits of an affluent society.

(Arnstein, 1969, p217)

Arnstein identified eight layers of participation (known as 'Arnstein's Ladder of Participation'; see Table 10.1) with local power increasing as participation increased and manipulation increasing as participation decreased.

Table 10.1 Arnheim's Ladder

Level	Type of participation	Nature of the experience
8	**Citizen control**	Degrees of citizen power
7	**Delegated power**	'
6	**Partnership**	'
5	**Placation**	Degrees of tokenism
4	**Consultation**	'
3	**Informing**	'
2	**Therapy**	Non-participation
1	**Manipulation**	'

Although often labelled as participation, activity at levels 1 and 2 is clearly not this at all. These levels can often be seen as attempts at public relations to gain support, perhaps through leaflets and the media, for decisions that already have been made. The activities at levels 3, 4 and 5 involve a greater degree of citizen involvement but the purpose of the exercise is, argues Arnstein, mostly to inform citizens through leaflets and public meetings, rather than effectively engage them in a real debate about decision-making. At levels 6, 7 and 8 citizens either have equal power with government bodies (level 6) or have decisions delegated to them (level 7). At the top level citizens have taken absolute control over the service or resources in question. These higher levels of participation are quite rare.

David Wilcox (1995) has adapted Arnstein's ladder and refocused it to practice within the UK. He agrees with Arnstein on the basic levels of *information* and *consultation* and then proposes three levels of partnership. Interestingly, and reflecting on the UK, he does not really focus on notions of full citizen power. Even so his three partnership levels of *deciding together*, *acting together* and *supporting independent community initiatives*, do broaden Arnstein's partnership category.

At fieldwork level there continues to be debate on the legitimacy of participation. Some of the questions often raised here are whether local community organisations want to become that involved with the decision making and responsibilities of local service providers, whether becoming involved in this way incorporates local groups into the establishment systems, and what the opportunity costs are of such involvement (by opportunity cost we mean that if you do one thing the opportunity to do something else, which actually might be more useful, is lost).

ACTIVITY *10.2*

Think of a participation exercise/event in which you have been involved. Identify where it is positioned in Arnstein's Ladder.

- *Why was it conducted at that level?*

- *Who decided this?*

- *In retrospect how participative was it?*

- *Was the conclusion of the participation expected or planned in advance?*

- *How else might the participation event been conducted to involve people more effectively?*

The term 'participation' is used by many people to mean a wide range of things. The process of analysis is crucial if we are to involve local people in processes that are meaningful otherwise we can unwittingly add to people's exploitation through tokenistic processes.

The view from the developing world

For development workers and NGOs it became clear during the 1980s and 1990s that the traditional approach to development was failing to work. Arundhati Roy's case study into the failure of large-scale dam and irrigation projects in India (*The Cost of Living*, 1999) and Sainath's book (*Everybody Loves a Good Drought*, 1999) on the failure of rural development are two early and notable examples illustrating this failure both in local practice, and also in policy and systems approach to change. Simply put, top-down and external expert-led development does not work. This is just as true for similar approaches for communities in the UK.

The change in analysis is illustrated well by Carolyn Jones (1996). Table 10.2 summarises the traditional development paradigm. As can be seen it combines an implicit belief in the

superiority of Western academic and technical expertise, with an almost dismissive approach to local people and local knowledge.

Table 10.2 The traditional development model (Jones, 1996)

Experts know the solution	*Communities* do not know the solution
Communities are the problem	*Experts* are the solution

From this change in analysis of how to proceed development workers began to develop bottom-up, participatory development models that sought to link external expertise to the recognition and valuing of local knowledge. Some of the early models became known as Rapid Rural Appraisal (RRA). Over time these models were refined and have become known as Participative Rapid Appraisal or PRA.

PRA has become for many NGOs the default development model. This is due in part to the ideological preference of working with, and valuing the knowledge of, local people. The other reason is that it works. Today PRA-based projects are being widely applied in the majority of countries across the world. It is used in developed as well as developing countries, in both urban and rural contexts, and in large- and small-scale operations. In the UK examples of PRA work can currently be found in community health projects, environmental work, self-help schemes, and community regeneration activities.

The revised model places local expertise and knowledge at the centre of the development process. External expertise can assist local people, but cannot do the work for or without them.

Table 10.3 Development model (Jones, 1996)

Communities know the solution	*Experts* do not know the solution
External influences are the problem	*Communities* are the solution

One criticism of PRA is that it often focuses on using local people to identify needs, but then falls back on established agencies, systems and power structures to meet those needs, or not, as the case may be. Often this is less a criticism of PRA than the result of a flawed application of the method by poorly trained practitioners.

In response to these criticisms there have been various changes to the model. It is now useful to conceptualise it as PLA (that is, Participatory Learning for Action), as this stresses that the purpose of the activity is to identify needs, develop new knowledge and take action for change. In this manifestation participatory work comes close to the Freirean cycle of reflection – vision – planning – action. In practice there can often be convergence between the Freirean and PLA approaches. In addition development work will take place at a higher level of Arnstein's Ladder with some transfer of power and agenda setting to local communities.

However, this is not just the application of technique. Freire reminds us that people in development situations will be constrained by limited boundary situations and distracted in their understanding of issues through naive consciousness. People in local communities can only make an effective contribution to development if involved in a developmental process. In one sense this seems obvious. Yet the practice in the youth and community field in the UK is often the opposite of this, where people are selected to join in what passes for 'focus groups' or 'community conferences'. As Arnstein might have said, this is less participation, more manipulation.

A broader critique comes from Cooke and Kothari (2001) who claim that PRA is just another method for incorporating local communities into a neoliberal development agenda, and that it talks the language of empowerment but is essentially a disempowering activity. Sometimes PRA is just that. This is true of all development methods. As Freire has said, methods can be used for liberation or domination – it all depends on the ideology and competence of the practitioners. In Gramscian terms development work can tie communities into the dominant hegemony, or create local organic intellectuals to build counter-hegemony. For further discussion, and a refutation of this critique of participative methodologies, see Hickey and Hohan (2004).

Carolyn Jones (1996) also picks up on the importance of ideological understanding and purpose of the development worker. In everyday practice, she suggests, workers should ask themselves:

- whose reality counts;
- whose knowledge counts;
- whose criteria and values count;
- whose appraisal counts ;
- whose analysis counts;
- whose plans count; and
- whose monitoring and evaluation count.

If workers adopt a participative approach to their work then the model of practice will shift from:

dominance	to	facilitation;
a closed approach	to	an open approach;
tedium	to	fun;
individual views	to	group discussions;
verbal methods	to	visual methods;
absolute methodologies	to	comparative methodologies;
valuing averages	to	valuing diversity.

The guru of PRA and PLA is Robert Chambers. He has written a summary of the practice so far. This account – *PRA to PLA and Pluralism: Practice and Theory* (2007) – is recommended to youth and community workers.

ACTIVITY 10.3

Carolyn Jones poses questions for workers engaged in participatory work:

- *whose reality counts;*

- *whose knowledge counts;*

- *whose criteria and values count;*

- *whose appraisal counts;*

- *whose analysis counts;*

- *whose plans count; and*

- *whose monitoring and evaluation count.*

What answers do you get to these questions in your own practice?

What answers do you get to these questions in your agency' practice?

A model of participatory practice

The question this leads us to is: 'How can youth and community workers apply these participatory techniques to practice?'

PRA or PLA activity can be undertaken by a Freirean or other community-based group or organisation. What is required is a grouping of people who are committed to developing new knowledge and understanding about their community. Armed with this knowledge communities are better equipped to identify required changes and the process of change. They will also have data and arguments to use for grant applications and for negotiation with external organisations and agencies.

It is for this group, often called a learning team, to identify the knowledge they need to develop. External expertise is likely to be required to facilitate the collection and analysis of data. However, it is essential to build in the principles of participation and for the key decisions to be made by community members.

There are many handbooks available to assist youth and community workers in facilitating community members through this exploratory learning agenda – these are listed at the end of this chapter.

CASE STUDY

Participative planning

A long-standing community group became frustrated with the kind of support they were receiving from local workers. Over the past ten years the group had been involved in community consultations and community conferences, had sent representatives to several partnerships, and had received training and grants to deliver a range of predetermined local services.

The group felt that they were always receiving things designed and planned by external agencies. They had participated in a variety of ways, but always with little power and not much influence over key decisions or what happened. The group wanted to take more control of their own affairs and have more influence over the local area.

The starting point for the group was to take a fresh look at the local community. Members of the group and other local people organised themselves into a learning team. The first activity was to undertake a transect walk across the local area. Each person made notes and took photographs as they walked. The idea was for people to think about and record what was significant about the area for them.

The material was used to create a wall-sized map with annotations and photographs. The content of the map was then discussed in a series of sessions. Each session was focused on a different grouping within the community. People made notes on sticky notes and added them to the wall. After these sessions had taken place the learning team examined the much-amended map and identified key themes for further work. The themes fell into a number of headings: road safety, personal safety, opportunities for young people, and local shops. Four new learning groups were set up and everyone who had been involved up until then was asked to join a group of their choice. With the exception of the theme of young people, external agencies had never discussed these themes locally.

The four thematic groups worked through a process where the issues were discussed in depth, and carried out visioning exercises to explore possibilities. Only after this process had been completed did the group explore local authorities' and partnerships' views, and discuss with local workers. This was an important sequence of events as it enabled the group to identify their own issues and equip themselves with significant knowledge and understanding. Once in this position they could participate with local agencies on a more powerful basis; in effect they moved themselves from the bottom of Arnstein's Ladder towards the top. Workers and agencies had to respond to community-generated initiatives and demands. Although difficult at times, a more genuine partnership relationship can be created this way.

The role of the worker supporting the group through the stages of the work was to: facilitate, provide basic training in skills and offer support as required. All decisions were made by the group.

From reviewing practice in the UK, Drysdale and Purcell (2001) identified a range of methods including:

- neighbourhood maps;
- life maps;
- issue maps;
- resource maps;

- power maps;

- storytelling; and

- tree of life.

These techniques are seldom applied individually. No single form of data collection can give us a meaningful insight into the life, needs and issues of a community. In research terms we need to 'triangulate' or, even better, to develop a holistic understanding of a question. Which combination of methods to use depends of course on local circumstances, personal preferences and the question under consideration. The research should be participative, with local people trained and supported to undertake the data collection themselves.

What is not here are the default 'semi-structured interviews' or so-called 'focus groups'. Done well these methods can be very powerful. However, fieldwork practice is often poor, with questions being poorly thought out. Usually, paid workers are the researchers, with local people locked into the position of being merely the objects of investigation. Sometimes this is called participation because local people participated in the interviews and groups, but such an approach would feature on a very low rung on Arnstein's Ladder.

Drysdale and Purcell describe the first of these methods in the following way:

> **Neighbourhood maps:** *A good starting activity is to invite people to draw or create maps of their communities, or their lives (when working with communities of interest). This has the benefit of helping people identify what are the important areas of their lives, what might be the potential problems or concerns, who is important to them and what kind of support/threat might be expected from them. This exercise can be undertaken with a wide variety of groups from school children to elders. Maps can be drawn indoors, but it can be most effective if it is compiled by a group of people walking through their community.*

> (Drysdale and Purcell, 2001, pp70–87)

Having created the map, participants can be asked to discuss:

- What do they see as difficulties for them?

- Where are they located in the map?

- Do they feel that their needs are met within the area?

- What are the gaps?

- What agencies are involved in the area – which are helpful and which are not?

Life maps: These can take two forms: a description of how people came to be in their current position, or a network diagram that helps people identify what difficulties and issues are in their lives. This exercise is best done with individuals, and then snowballed into general themes. Individual maps may need to remain confidential.

Issue maps: These can be made, for example, for crime spots, caring need timetables, gaps in child care provision (area or times), access to shops, or leisure facilities.

Resource maps: These can be made to show physical resources within an area. They can also map the specialist knowledge and skills of organisations, workers and community organisations.

Power maps: These can also be used to see who holds power over the use of resources, ownership of land and facilities, or the informal power relationships within a community.

Use of maps: By identifying what changes they would want to make, people can begin to understand that their situations are influenced by external agencies, or institutional and structural oppression such as poverty, poor educational opportunities, and housing allocation policies. To achieve this you need to facilitate people in thinking about the various agencies (or individuals) who are in the area and what their relationships are to them. They also need to think about the relationships between these agencies.

These maps can be presented in a variety of forms, for example:

- *Photographs:* Digital cameras are an invaluable tool because they allow instant replay for discussion. The images can also be easily and cheaply used for posters, displays, and other forms of computer production.

- *Drawings:* These can be very powerful for expressing feeling. They also overcome people's inhibitions about literacy. They are also an essential approach when working with young children.

- *Diagrams:* These are useful to make links between diverse elements. For example, flow charts can show how decisions are made.

- *Montage:* These can use images from newspapers and magazines as well as photographs and drawings produced locally.

ACTIVITY **10.4**

Select from the following list of investigative tools:

- *neighbourhood maps;*
- *issue maps;*
- *resource maps;*
- *power maps.*

Use this tool to map an aspect of a community, as a worker viewing the community.

Repeat the exercise with community members.

Compare the results.

What does this suggest to you?

Storytelling: This is another activity that can get people talking about their lives, their needs and their dreams. There are a number of ways to encourage this to happen.

- Choose soap characters who remind people of themselves.

- Explore pictures, music or other creative art they think says something about their own experiences.

- Ask people to remember street games and stories that say something about their lives.

- Make up stories about people like themselves.

- Tell their own story of, for example, oppression, stress, or happiness.

People need to feel comfortable, so they should only be encouraged to share as much as they feel comfortable to speak about. Nobody should feel coerced into participating.

These stories can then be translated into plays, drawings, human sculptures, models made from rubbish, and so on. You need to have some knowledge of what people will take the risk to try. Most people will have a go if the facilitator is encouraging, sets it up as being a fun activity and is patient.

Storytelling can also be about the area that people live in, or the situation that people share, for instance nursery schools, older persons' accommodation, disability or poverty.

Tree of Life: In this method people are asked to draw the tree of their own life, in which:

- the roots of the tree are the family and the influences that have shaped their life;

- the trunk is the structure of their life today – their family, job, community or organisations which are important to them;

- the leaves are their information sources, newspapers, community radio stations, friends and contacts;

- the buds are their hopes, dreams and aspirations;

- the fruits are their achievements.

The above methods tend to explore micro-level and personal questions. As such they work very well with Freirean groups who are often also exploring questions of self development. Sometimes, though, we need to pose wider questions about the nature of the community rather than individual or group experiences of it. These macro-level questions can fit within a Gramscian analysis of the community.

Barr, Hashagan and Purcell (1996b) have produced a useful guide to exploring macro-level questions of community concern. As above, local people can be trained and supported to explore these questions. The authors suggest the following framework of questions may be useful to develop a broader understanding of an area:

- *History:* How has the area or interest community come to be as it is? What historical events colour perceptions that people have of themselves and their neighbourhood or interest group? This information is often important in appreciating the degree of difficulty that may be involved in achieving change. Here there is likely to be an emphasis on consulting existing records and informal interviewing of key informants.

- *Environment:* How is space used/abused? Not only physical layout but occupancy density and condition of environment, including housing, roads and public space, are critical. Who is responsible for what aspects of the environment? In this context observation is likely to be a particularly important tool.

- *The residents:* How many are there? Where do they come from? How long have they been there? What do they do? How poor/affluent are they? What conditions do they live in? What are their values and traditions? What are their demographic characteristics? What services do they use? How far do they perceive themselves as sharing common interests? and so on. It should be noted that there are likely to be identifiable sub-groups within any population. Their relationships may be a source of tension. Much data will already be available from a variety of sources to supply this information. It will probably need to be supplemented by observation and by questioning.

- *Organisations:* There will usually be a wide range of organisations functioning in a neighbourhood or in relation to particular interest communities. These include: commercial organisations, public sector agencies of local and central government, religious bodies, voluntary agencies, and organisations created and owned by the community itself. Some will be located in the area while others will service it from outside. Who are they, what do they do, what resources do they have, and what influence do they have on neighbourhood affairs? Such organisations control resources that are potentially of vital importance in the achievement of change. Questioning will be a primary means of establishing who is involved but the exploration of their role is likely to be facilitated as much by access to agency documentation and observations of interactions with the community.

- *Communications:* This dimension is particularly important to the consideration of process. The researcher needs to know how information is passed on both formally and informally. The latter is often most significant but hardest to discover – who are the opinion leaders, what are the key networks in operation in the community, and how are they sustained? How effective is communication between local community interests and external agencies? A combination of informal questioning and observation is likely to be relevant for this purpose.

- *Power and leadership:* It is crucial to know who has power and how it is used. This relates both to the external organisations operating in the community and to the community itself. It requires understanding the role of politicians, local and central government officers of all kinds, religious leaders, business and commercial leaders as well as understanding the politics and power struggles within the community and its internal organisations. Records of events (particularly in local media), informal questioning and observation are all likely to be of importance.

ACTIVITY **10.5**

The Community Partnership Centre at the University of Tennessee developed a checklist to determine the relative health of a community for development purposes.

Table 10.4 Healthy and unhealthy communities (adapted from Community Partnership Centre, 2000)

Healthy Community	Unhealthy Community
Optimism	Cynicism
Focus on unification	Focus on division
Consensus building	Polarisation
'We're in this together'	'Not in my back yard'
Solving problems	Holding grudges
Interdependence	Parochialism
Win – win solutions	Win – lose solutions
Trust	Questioning motives
Politics of substance	Politics of personality
Diversity	Exclusion
Challenge ideas	Challenge people
Problem solvers	Blockers
Taking personal responsibility	Other person's responsibility
Listening	Attacking
Focus on the future	Focus on the past
Sharing power	Hoarding power
We can do it	Nothing works

How would you assess the community in which you work in terms of the above characteristics?

What strategies can you adopt to help community members move from the unhealthy to healthy category?

Note: This task can be completed as an individual exercise. It also works well as a team exercise and as a workshop involving both local workers and community members.

C H A P T E R   R E V I E W

In this chapter we have discussed the meaning of participation, and how this understanding has changed in the light of experience in the developing world. We then explored examples, drawn from practice handbooks, on how to apply participation at both the micro- and macro-levels.

FURTHER READING

Specific references to useful practice guides and handbooks have been made in the chapter. In particular we recommend the following:

Archer, D and Cottingham, S (1996) *Reflect Mother Manual: Regenerated Freirean Literacy Through Empowering Community Techniques.* London: ActionAid.

Chambers, R (2002) *Participatory Workshops: A Sourcebook of 21 Sets of Ideas and Activities.* Sterling, Vancouver: Earthscan.

Chapter 11
Theatre of the Oppressed

CHAPTER OBJECTIVES

This chapter explores a drama-based approach to the popular education aims of developing critical consciousness and collective action developed by Augusto Boal. In particular it examines three of his main techniques – Image Theatre, Forum Theatre and Invisible Theatre – and how they can be effectively used in the context of youth and community work.

This approach provides useful theoretical and practical tools to enable workers to successfully undertake the key role in youth work which is to:

> [e]nable young people to develop holistically, working with them to facilitate their personal, social and educational development, to enable them to develop their voice, influence and place in society and to reach their full potential.

> (LLUK, 2008, p3)

It will also enable workers to fulfil Key Role B: Encourage people to work with and learn from each other, in particular to *promote and support learning from practice and experience* (PAULO, 2003, p30).

Background

Augusto Boal, born in Brazil in 1931, took the ideas of Paulo Freire and translated them into a revolutionary form of theatre. His thinking, which was first expressed in his seminal book *The Theatre of the Oppressed*, was developed in the context of a repressive political regime, high inflation, strikes and riots from the 1950s to the 1970s. The influence of Freire on his thinking and practice began when he was working in a Freirean-based literacy programme in Peru in 1973.

Theatre of the Oppressed

The Theatre of the Oppressed is the umbrella term for the drama-based techniques which Augusto Boal developed to work with people in order to develop critical consciousness. It develops an environment where people can discover what their creative capacity is and to reacquire his or her own capability to create. It opens a dialogue between people where they can put themselves in the place of the other – real encounters, where everybody can see their own image reflected through the eye of the other (Santos, 2008).

This approach offers everyone the aesthetic means to analyse their past, in the context of their present, and subsequently to invent their future, without waiting for it. It helps human beings to recover a language they already possess – we learn how to live in society by playing theatre. We learn how to feel by feeling, how to think by thinking, how to act by acting. Theatre of the Oppressed is rehearsal for reality. It is therefore an approach which enables people to explore their lived reality, critically examine it in the light of other people's perceptions, and experience what it means to act and feel differently.

The three techniques outlined below are applicable in a range of youth and community work contexts. We would encourage you to adapt and experiment with them in order to find an approach which suits you in the particular context you are working in. They all involve differing levels of risk, as most community development interventions do, but when they work well, they are fun, energising and potentially life-changing for the people involved and the communities in which they live and work.

Image Theatre

Image Theatre is the basic vocabulary of all the various branches of the Theatre of the Oppressed, from simple techniques such as Image of the Word (where participants are asked to sculpt themselves into a statue representing their reaction to a given word), through to more complex techniques such as Image of Transition (where the technique studies the possibilities of change). Image Theatre harnesses the simplest form of self-representation to arrive at the deepest form of debate. The power of this work, for me, lies in the way in which an image can by-pass words and avoids the problems of verbal debate (Poulter, 1995).

Participants are asked to depict a particular feeling, experience or issue as it is in the present using only their own bodies in a static representation. Participants are encouraged to act and move rather than to discuss and think about what they are going to do. Boal's thinking behind this technique is that use of the body as the medium of communication helps participants to think outside the normal constraints and blockages of language and gain new insights into the issue under examination. Participants can then rearrange fellow participants until they have a picture that represents the issue accurately. This process is repeated until a general consensus is found, in which all are content that the image is an accurate representation.

In the second phase of the process participants are asked to create the ideal image of the issue, again only using their bodies to form a sculpture. Finally, an 'image of transition' is created which displays an interim situation between the reality of the oppression and the ideal image, to develop realist actions which might lead to change. At the end of each phase of the technique the group can be posed questions about what is happening and why, in a similar way to the questioning procedure when using Freirean codes.

This is a useful technique in a wide range of situations, for example working with a well-established group who feel they have lost focus and direction. The technique provides a safe way of representing and then exploring their 'stuckness' without blaming or defending individual positions. Phase two enables them to recapture the vision of what they want to achieve and how they want to work together and the final phase offers a creative way to begin a process of action planning for change.

ACTIVITY **11.1**

With a group of fellow students/workers, explore the use of Image Theatre.

- *Identify a common issue of concern.*
- *Half of the group, using only your bodies, must now represent how this issue is experienced by you at this point.*
- *The other half of the group repositions people until they feel they have accurately represented the issue.*
- *The whole group then discusses what they have seen, how it felt and what it helps them to understand about the issue.*

You will have discovered that through this approach which does not rely wholly on language, a wider range of issues and feelings are identified and explored. The role of the worker in this is to push for deeper analysis of the issue, allowing the group to identify their own answers and solutions.

Forum Theatre

Forum Theatre is an interactive process involving actors and 'spect-actors' (active audience members) in order to explore issues of oppression and how they can be overcome in the lives of the participants. An audience is shown a short play in which the main protagonist encounters an oppression or obstacle which s/he is unable to overcome. There is then a brief discussion amongst the audience about the issues in the play – what was attempted and why it didn't work. The play is restarted. Whenever a spect-actor feels the protagonist might usefully have tried a different strategy, s/he can stop the action, take the protagonist's place, and try his or her idea. The other characters in the piece will react as they feel their characters would react, i.e. they will make it realistically difficult for any new tactic to succeed; but if an idea works, the intervening spect-actor can win, the game is not rigged (**http://cardboardcitizens.org.uk/ theatre_of_the_oppressed.php**).

The act of transforming is transformatory. The spect-actor comes on stage and transforms the images that they see and do not like – they transform them into images they like and desire, images of a just, convivial society – and in the act of taking the stage, they transform themselves into a sculptor, musician, poet – in sum, entering the stage and showing their will in action, being the actor, being the protagonist, the spect-actor transforms themself into a citizen!

Cardboard Citizens

*Cardboard Citizens (**www.cardboardcitizens.org.uk**/) audition and hire four company members – trained actors with experience with homelessness to perform in the play along with Cardboard Citizens' Associate Artist, Terry O'Leary, who plays the role of the Joker.*

They perform short plays in hostels based on difficulties faced by a migrant worker, a young person fresh out of care, and a hostel worker. At the end of each play, the Joker facilitates a discussion with the audience about the challenges faced by the characters in the play and asks them what they might have done differently to improve the outcome for the protagonist. After this discussion, the plays are restarted, but now audience members can stop the performance, take the place of the actors and try out their idea of what the protagonist might have done differently. These experiences generate a unique sense of solidarity and empowerment among hostel residents, and inspire them to reach and recognise their potential.

After each show, trained mentoring actors spend time talking to homeless clients and arrange one-to-one follow up meetings, ensuring that the inspiration generated by the performance is translated into some form of positive action.

Split into two groups – actors and spect-actors.

The group of actors spends 15 minutes planning an improvisation around the theme of tackling racism. They perform the short play and the spect-actors discuss with them what they have seen.

The play is then re-run. This time at points where the spect-actors think an actor could have said or done something differently, they stop the action and take their place and try their alternative.

This process can be continued until the group feel they have come up with a workable solution to the issue.

Invisible Theatre

Invisible Theatre is a play which is developed by a group and then performed in a public place without the public realising that it is a performance. It is a risky form, because the audience take it for reality, and thus the participants have to be ready for anything! The focus of the performance is to elicit discussion and debate around an issue of social justice.

The actors will have a script but improvisation will arise due to the interaction of the public. Often the performance will include members of the group pretending to be passersby.

Invisible Theatre examples

Three of us visited a local supermarket. One played a newly released 'Asylum' seeker, supported by 'Concerned', the third a prejudiced character. We got a few cheap goods and queued at the checkout. The ex-detainee realised she couldn't buy everything and 'Concerned' offered to lend her money. The third character, also queuing, overheard and protested. They argued as they waited. 'Concerned' said her friend had to flee and couldn't work, the other countered, 'She's left her people in the lurch, we can't afford to take in everyone. . . .' The ex-detainee urged quiet, she didn't want trouble. The scene generated a lot of interest. No-one from the public joined in but a small group gathered and listened intently.

(Norris, 1997)

In order to raise consciousness about sexual harassment, three actors – two women and a man – board an underground train. The actresses start ogling the actor and touching his bottom. A scripted quarrel ensues between the women and the man. The passengers join in the scene by commenting and intervening. A discussion ensues about how sexual harassment can victimise both men and women. Through their involvement, spectators engage in a learning process in which they are free to decide for themselves which stand they want to take.

(Moorthy, undated)

ACTIVITY *11.3*

Devise an example of Invisible Theatre which could explore issues of consumerism in a shopping mall.

- *What might be the impact?*
- *Would you need to do any follow-up work with people affected by the drama?*
- *Do you think this is a good way to deal with the issue?*

CHAPTER REVIEW

The Theatre of the Oppressed offers a range of ways to help people explore their past, present and future. It provides an abbreviated experience of transformed social relationships; people can feel what it would be like to live in a world where they have a voice and power to act. The ability to transcend the boundaries of language opens up creative spaces for transforming ways of both thinking and acting and can recharge the emotional reservoirs of people involved in social change. Finally, it is fun and challenging and acts as a real contrast to much of our committee-based forms of practice.

The theoretical background and application of Boal's approach are outlined in this, his most influential work.

Boal, A (1992) *Games for Actors and Non-actors.* London: Routledge.

Boal's other works include:

Boal, A (1994) *The Rainbow of Desire: The Boal Method of Theatre and Therapy.* London: Routledge.

Boal, A (1998) *The Legislative Theatre: Using Performance to Make Politics.* London: Routledge.

Boal, A (2001) *Hamlet and the Baker's Son: My Life in Theatre and Politics.* London: Routledge.

Theatre of the Oppressed Organisation:
www.theatreoftheoppressed.org/en/index.php?useFlash=0

Pedagogy & Theatre of the Oppressed: **www.ptoweb.org/home.html**

Essential Dissent – Nightwind (video): **http://essentialdissent.blogspot.com/2008/11/
nightwind-theatre-of-oppressed-part-1.html**

Theatre of the Oppressed on Wikipedia: **http://en.wikipedia.org/wiki/Theatre_of_the_Oppressed**

Experiments in forum theatre – young people and racism:
www.youtube.com/watch?v=sYeEMpD_nbI&feature=related

Theatre of the Oppressed and AIDS awareness in Mozambique:
www.youtube.com/watch?v=aG3iyi-CEwA

Chapter 12
Practice examples

Case example 1: Youth worker

Background

Lorna is a youth worker who organises a young women's group. This is a two-hour weekly meeting of 16- to 18-year-old girls who are all still at school. To date the group have been undertaking traditional youth work activity such as group-building games, guest speakers, and social trips to McDonalds, ten-pin bowling, and so on. Previously they have received 'off-the-shelf' informal education packages from the youth work team. Usually these packages run for six sessions and have included first aid and healthy eating.

The group are becoming dissatisfied with these activities as they feel they are too mature for what they perceive to be children's activities. Lorna wants to engage the group in more important work.

Popular education response

The group could explore their collective interests and needs. Lorna's role is to facilitate this and not impose her own ideas on the group.

The young women could bring in a range of magazines and select images from them that they think comment on women of their age group. Each image is discussed by the group. From these discussions Lorna's job is to identify emerging themes. These themes are listed and the group select the three most important/interesting ones for further exploration. In the following weeks and months each of the themes is worked on for as long as required to enable the group to identify the issues contained within it and to work through what response they choose to make. In practice this could be a few weeks or several months.

Once a theme is selected (*generative theme*) the young women are asked to bring in for the next meeting any object they wish that relates to the theme and that they wish to talk about. This could be more pictures, short articles, poems, personal mementoes, etc. (these objects are *codes*).

At this meeting Lorna ensures that each object is discussed in turn. As the discussion develops the issues relating to the theme will emerge. Lorna has a critical role in facilitating these discussions and making sure key points of concern are recorded (*reflective phase*).

The following meeting should focus on the key issues and realistically explore what the group wants to do about them. This of course is for the group to decide and many things may emerge: finding out more information, thinking about family and personal relationships, initiating/joining in related local activities (*vision* phase).

Future meetings will move from exploring the issues, to deciding what is to be done (*planning* phase) to *taking personal and collective actions* and then *reviewing* what has been learnt and achieved.

Case example 2: Detached youth worker

Background

As a detached youth worker in an inner city housing estate, Leroy has made contact with an informal group of young men. The ages of the group runs from 16 to the early 20s. Most of the group are not in education or employment. Although not directly observed by Leroy, he knows the group are engaged in low-level drug misuse and petty crime and that several young men carry knives.

Popular education response

It is essential to recognise that the young men are making what appears to them to be rational life choices, albeit from a position of naive consciousness. They do not expect to have a career or to move into better housing or away from the estate. Their group is strongly bonded and provides personal support and, they claim, protection.

The young men will not move from this position unless they reframe their personal identities and develop a positive belief that both change and a better life are possible. One approach is for Leroy to start discussion with the young men to get them to reflect on what they like/dislike about their current lives and to develop a vision of a better life. From listening to what the group says Leroy needs to identify a generative theme that resonates with the young men. From this he could identify a person (of the same background, class, ethnicity, etc.) and use him as a code from which the group can critically explore the theme. Leroy's objective is to facilitate the young men to see that personal and collective change is possible. Some of this may be quite small but it is a first step to changing their self-perception and boundary situation. Over time the group will identify, plan and initiate action to move themselves towards a better life.

Case example 3: Health education worker

Background

Andy is working with a community-based health group. His remit is to work with low-income families and contribute to improving the general level of health in the community. The group has around 20 members, and between six and nine people turn up to a meeting. The group has had many visiting speakers on a range of topics: basic exercise, power walking, cooking on a budget, giving up smoking, etc. Overall, Andy feels that people are not committed to the group and little is being achieved.

Popular education response

For this group to succeed it is important that they define for themselves what they understand by good health and why it is important to them individually. Having professionals telling you where you are failing seldom achieves a sustained and positive response.

Andy could use one of the group sessions to explore what people understand by good health. As in Case Example 1 he could ask people to bring in an object that people associate with health. These objects can be discussed and themes will emerge. Just like Lorna above, these themes can be unpacked so that group members explore their own notions of health, what stops them from achieving better health and what they want to do about it.

A range of proposals for action may emerge. For example negotiating reduced subscriptions to a local health centre/swimming pool/swimming lessons, or collective support to take exercise such as weekly walks together.

Case example 4: Parent support worker

Background

Mona works with a group of young single mothers with children either under school age or attending primary school. Some of the women are in relationships of various kinds. Only two of the women work (part time and low paid). The group has been created to develop parenting skills and all of the women have been 'encouraged' by welfare or health professionals to attend. The group mostly sits around chatting whilst the children play in a separate room. Mona realises that simply telling the women what they should do as parents is unlikely to succeed. Input to the groups by health visitors and a play worker have not led to any obvious change in parenting activity.

Popular education response

The starting point could be working with the women to explore a range of personal issues: perhaps their own experience of being a child, their current feeling/identity of being a parent, hopes and expectations for their child. Where to start depends of course on the women themselves. As always Mona needs to listen to the women to identify a generative theme from which she can bring a code to the group. From exploring the code the women will engage in the same process as Leroy's group; it is possible for their hopes for their child to be realised, they can find more fulfilment and satisfaction from being a parent, and the women can strengthen their identities as mothers. For each of these ideals, clear objectives have to be identified, plans made to get there, actions taken and reflected upon.

As in all of the case examples, change is most likely to happen when people can critically reflect upon their situation, understand the context of why their life is currently like it is and have clear realistic strategies for personal and collective change.

Section 3
Resources

Internet resources

This is a collection of useful web sites. The addresses were correct at time of writing (December 2009).

Action sites

Adbusters: www.adbusters.org
An innovative site turning advertising and consumerism against itself. The site describes itself as a 'global network of artists, activists, writers, pranksters, students, educators and entrepreneurs who want to advance the new social activist movement of the information age'.

Culture Jamming: www.abrupt.org/CJ/
Creative play on consumerism and advertising. Useful for stimulating ideas for creative and challenging publicity.

Urban 75: www.urban75.com/Action/index.html
Very extensive UK site and the first port of call for alternative campaigns. Urban 75 brings you the latest news from actions, demos and events, along with background features and resources. Also has a good football section!

GreenNet: www.gn.apc.org/
GreenNet describes itself as an ethical ISP that has been connecting people and groups who work for peace, the environment, gender equality and human rights since 1986.

Jubilee Debt Campaign: www.jubileedebtcampaign.org.uk/
Campaigns to change the global economic system and to put people first. Useful collection of educational resources to explain international debt and finance from a variety of perspectives.

Reclaim the Streets: http://rts.gn.apc.org/
Describes itself as a 'direct action network for global and local social-ecological revolution(s) to transcend hierarchical and authoritarian society (capitalism included), and still be home in time for tea . . .' Provides practical information about street parties and other activities.

Relief Web: www.reliefweb.int/
A resource site for the humanitarian community. Provides up-to-date information on international emergencies.

Undercurrents: www.undercurrents.org/
UK-based alternative video-based news, video training service, and news on various campaigns in the UK.

Library sites

Infed: www.infed.org/
Extensive range of articles and links on informal education and social learning.

SOSIG: www.intute.ac.uk/socialsciences/
Search page of the Social Science Information Gateway, a useful source for academic information.

Media sites

The Anatomy of Power: www.davidsmail.info/anpower.htm
A useful introductory site that summarises a range of critical thinkers from Thomas Paine through Marx to Illich.

Bureau of Public Secrets: www.bopsecrets.org/
Off-the-wall collection of radical texts.

Noam Chomsky: www.chomsky.info/
The collected works of Noam Chomsky: a radical reworking of American imperialism and media.

The Economist: www.economist.com/
The world according to the capitalist orthodoxy of globalisation.

History of Ideas: www.dcu.ie/~comms/philosophy/ph-texts.htm
A personal collection of Marxist material.

Marxists Internet Archive: www.marxists.org/
Very extensive Internet resource on Marxist writers and history.

Postmodern: www.euro.net/mark-space/Postmodern.html
Diverse selection of resources by postmodernist and related thinkers and writers.

Red Pepper: www.redpepper.org.uk/
UK left-of-centre magazine.

John Pilger articles: http://www.johnpilger.com/
Archive and video material of the crusading journalist.

Theory.org: www.theory.org.uk/index.htm
Extensive material relating to popular culture and social theory. Follow this link for Gramsci-focused resources: www.theory.org.uk/ctr-gram.htm

Resource sites

Catalyst Centre: www.catalystcentre.ca
Canadian Popular Education resource centre: online papers, bibliography and other resources.

The Community Toolbox: http://ctb.ku.edu/en/
US-based site which claims to be the world's largest resource for building communities.

Eldis: www.eldis.org/
The international resource site for development policy, practice and research information.

Federation for Community Development Learning: www.fcdl.org.uk/
Training resource site for community development practice.

Freire Institute: www.freire.net
UK-based and globally focused site. Follow this link to find other Paulo Freire organisations: **www.freire.net/index.php/paulo-freire-organizations.html**

Lifelong Learning: www.open.ac.uk/lifelong-learning/index.html
The papers from the Open University Global Colloquium on Lifelong Learning.

National Youth Agency: www.nya.org.uk
The UK National Youth Agency home page.

NIACE: www.niace.org.uk/
The UK National Institute for Adult Continuing Education home page.

The Popular Education News: www.popednews.org/index.html
Monthly email on popular education, plus other resources.

PovertyNet: www.worldbank.org/poverty/index.htm
World Bank resources for poverty issues and development. Lots of technical reports and information.

United Nations Development Programme: www.undp.org/
The United Nations Development Programme reports on the current state of the developing world.

United Nations Human Rights: www.ohchr.org
Home page for the UN High Commission for Human Rights, explores rights issues on a global basis.

World Bank Resources: www.worldbank.org/html/extdr/showcase.htm
The World Bank Portal site.

References

Acosta, D (2007) CUBA: Popular education transforms women's lives. Available at: **www.ipsnews.net/news.asp?idnews=40124** (accessed 13 November 2009).

Alinsky, SD (1989) *Rules for Radicals: a Practical Primer for Realistic Radicals*. New York: Vintage Books.

Allman, P (2001) *Revolutionary Social Transformation: Democratic Hopes, Political Possibilities and Critical Education*. Westport, CT: Bergin & Garvey.

Amnesty International (2008) *The State of the World's Human Rights*. Available at: **www.thereport.amnesty.org/eng/Homepage** (accessed 13 November 2009).

Archer, D and Cottingham, S (1996) *Reflect Mother Manual: Regenerated Freirean Literacy through Empowering Community Techniques*. London: ActionAid.

Arnstein, SR (1969) A ladder of citizen participation. *Journal of the American Institute of Planners*, 35(4): 216–224.

Barr, A, Hamilton, R and Purcell, R (1996a) *Learning for Change: Community Education and Community Development*. London: Community Development Foundation.

Barr, A, Hashagan, S and Purcell, R (1996b) *Monitoring and Evaluation of Community Development in Northern Ireland*. Belfast: Voluntary Activities Unit, NI DHSS.

Batten, TR (1967) *The Non-Directive Approach in Group and Community Work*. Oxford: Oxford University Press.

Bibby, A (2001) Coin Street: Case study. Available at: **www.andrewbibby.com/socialenterprise/coin-street.html** (accessed 13 November 2009).

Boal, A (1992) *Games for Actors and Non-Actors*. London: Routledge.

Boal, A (1994) *The Rainbow of Desire: The Boal Method of Theatre and Therapy*. London: Routledge.

Boal, A (1998) *The Legislative Theatre: Using Performance to Make Politics*. London: Routledge.

Boal, A (2000) *The Theatre of the Oppressed*. London: Pluto Press.

Boal, A (2001) *Hamlet and the Baker's Son: My Life in Theatre and Politics*. London: Routledge.

Brenner, R (2006) Structure vs. conjuncture: The 2006 elections and rightward shift. *New Left Review*, 43: 33–59.

Brickell, P (2000) *People before Structures*. London: Demos.

Brookfield, S (1991) *Understanding and Facilitating Adult Learning: A Comprehensive Analysis of Principles and Effective Practices*. San Francisco: Jossey-Bass.

Brookfield, S (2004) Racializing and concretizing Gramsci in contemporary adult education practice. *Interchange*, 35(3): 375–384.

Brookfield, S (2005) *The Power of Critical Theory for Adult Learning and Teaching.* Maidenhead: Open University Press.

Burkhart, BY (2004) What Coyote and Thales can teach us: An outline of American Indian epistemology, in Waters, A (ed) *American Indian Thought: Philosophical Essays.* Oxford: Blackwell.

Carroll, W and Ratner, R (2001) Sustaining oppositional cultures in 'post-socialist times': A comparative study of three social movement organisations. *Sociology*, 35(3): 605–629.

CDP Inter-Project Editorial Team (1977) *Gilding the Ghetto.* London: CDP IIU.

CDP Inter-Project Editorial Team (1977) *The Costs of Industrial Change.* London: CDP IIU.

de Certeau, M (1984) *The Practice of Everyday Life*, tr. Rendall, S. Berkeley, CA: University of California Press.

Chambers, R (2002) *Participatory Workshops: A Sourcebook of 21 Sets of Ideas and Activities.* Sterling, Vancouver: Earthscan.

Chambers, R (2007) From PRA to PLA and pluralism: Practice and theory. *IDS Working Paper* 286. Brighton: Institute of Development Studies.

Clark, C (1993) Transformational learning. *New Directions for Adult and Continuing Education*, 57: 47–56.

Claude, RP (2000) *Popular Education for Human Rights: 24 Participatory Exercises for Teachers and Facilitators.* Cambridge, MA: HREA.

Cohen, A (2003) *The Symbolic Construction of Community.* London: Routledge.

Coit, K (1978) Local action, not citizen participation, in Tabb, W and Sawers, L (eds) *Marxism and the Metropolis.* Oxford: Oxford University Press.

Coleman, JS (1971) Conflicting theories of social change. *American Behavioral Scientist*, 14: 633–650.

Collins, DE (1977) *Paulo Freire: His Life, Works and Thought.* New York: Paulist Press.

Cooke, B and Kothari, U (2001) *Participation: The New Tyranny?* London: Zed Books.

Coin Street Community Builders (CSCB) (2009) There is another way on London's South Bank. Available at: **www.coinstreet.org/aboutus.aspx** (accessed 13 November 2009).

Daloz, L (1990) Slouching toward Bethlehem. *Continuing Higher Education*, 39(11): 2–9.

Dembour, M (2006) *Who Believes in Human Rights? Reflections on the European Convention.* Cambridge: Cambridge University Press.

Drysdale, J and Purcell, R (1999) Breaking the culture of silence: Group work and community development. *Group Work*, 11(3): 70–87.

Drysdale, J and Purcell, R (2001) *Reclaiming the Agenda: Participation in Practice.* Bradford: CWTC.

Duncombe, S (2002) *Cultural Resistance Reader.* London: Verso.

Field, J (2003) *Social Capital.* Routledge: London.

Foucault, M (1991) *The Foucault Reader: An Introduction to Foucault's Thought.* London: Penguin.

Freire, AMA and Macedo, D (eds) (1998) *The Paulo Freire Reader.* New York: Continuum.

Freire, P (1972) *Pedagogy of the Oppressed*. Harmondsworth: Penguin.

Freire, P (1976) *Education, the Practice of Freedom*. London: Writers and Readers Publishing Cooperative.

Freire, P (c1998) *Pedagogy of Hope: Reliving Pedagogy of the Oppressed*, Freire, AMA (notes), Barr, RR (tr). New York: Continuum.

Fritz, C (1982) *Because I Speak Cockney They Think I'm Stupid*. Newcastle: Association of Community Workers.

Gandhi, MK ([1927] 2007) *An Autobiography: Or the Story of My Experiments with Truth*, translated by Desai, M. London: Penguin.

Geertz, C (1975) *The Interpretation of Cultures*. London: Hutchinson.

Gillies, V and Edwards, R (2006) A qualitative analysis of parenting and social capital: Comparing the work of Coleman and Bourdieu. *Qualitative Sociology Review*, 2(2). Available at: **www.qualitativesociologyreview.org/ENG/archive_eng.php** (accessed 13 November 2009).

Gittell, M, Ortega-Bustamante, I and Steffy, T (2000) Social capital and social change: Women's community activism. *Urban Affairs Review*, 36: 123–147.

Grameen Bank (2009) Introduction. Available at: **www.grameen-info.org/index.php?option=com_content&task=view&id=16&Itemid=112** (accessed 13 November 2009).

Grameen Creative Lab (2009) Grameen Bank: The mother of Grameen Social Business. Available at: **www.grameencreativelab.com/live-examples/grameen-bank-the-mother-of-grameen-social-business.html** (accessed 13 November 2009).

Gramsci, A (1971) *Selections from the Prison Notebooks*. New York: International Publishers.

Grotius, H ([1625] 2005) *Rights of War and Peace*, edited by Tuck, R. Indianapolis: Liberty Fund.

Gulbenkian Committee (1968) *Community Work and Social Change*. London: Longman.

Hall, P (1952) *The Social Services of Modern England*. London: Routledge and Kegan Paul.

Hancock, JM (2006) Universal human rights: Claims by the Ogoni people of Nigeria and the paradox of cultural relativism. Paper presented at the annual meeting of the International Studies Association, Town & Country Resort and Convention Center, San Diego, California, USA. Available at: **www.allacademic.com/meta/p100631_index.html** (accessed 13 November 2009).

Henderson, P and Thomas, D (2002) *Skills in Neighbourhood Work*. London: Routledge and Kegan Paul.

Hickey, S and Hohan, G (2004) *Participation: From Tyranny to Transformation? Exploring New Approaches to Participation in Development*. London: Zed Books.

HMSO (1975) *Adult Education: The Challenge of Change* (The Alexander Report). London: The Stationery Office.

Hobbes, T ([1651] 2008) *Leviathan*, edited by Gaskin, J. Oxford: Oxford University Press.

Hope, A and Timmel, S (1984) *Training for Transformation Vol 3*. London: ITDG Publishing.

Hope, A and Timmel, S (1999) *Training for Transformation Vol 4*. London: ITDG Publishing.

Ife, J (2004) *Linking Community Development and Human Rights.* Deakin University, Australia: Community Development, Human Rights and the Grassroots Conference.

Ife, J and Fiske L (2006) Human rights and community work: Complementary theories and practices. *International Social Work,* 49: 297.

Illich, I (1973) *Tools for Conviviality.* New York: Harper & Row.

Illich, I (2005) *Disabling Professions.* London: Marion Boyars.

Jeffs, T and Smith, M (eds) (1990) *Young People, Inequality and Youth Work.* London: Macmillan.

Jesson, J and Newman, M (2004) Radical adult education and learning, in Foley, G (ed) *Understanding Adult Education and Training.* New South Wales: Allen & Unwin.

Jones, C (1996) *PRA in Central Asia: Coping with Change.* Brighton: IDS Sussex University.

Kelly, A and Sewell, S (1989) *With Heads, Hearts and Hands: Dimensions of Community Building.* Brisbane: Boolarong Press.

Kelman, C and Warwick, D (1978) The ethics of social interventions: Goals, means and consequences. *The Ethics of Social Intervention,* 3: 33).

Kincheloe, J (2008) *Critical Pedagogy.* New York: Peter Lang.

Ledwith, M (2005) *Community Development: A Critical Approach.* Bristol: Policy Press.

Lefebvre, H (1991) *The Production of Space.* Oxford: Wiley-Blackwell.

Lefebvre, H (2008) *The Critique of Everyday Life 1–3.* London: Verso.

LLUK (2008) *The National Occupational Standards for Youth Work.* London: Lifelong Learning UK.

Locke, J ([1690] 2002) *The Second Treatise of Government and a Letter Concerning Toleration.* New York: Dover Publications.

Lownd, P (undated) Freire's life and work: A brief biography of Paulo Freire. Available at: **www. paulofreireinstitute.org** (accessed 13 November 2009).

Luft, J and Ingham, H (1955) The Johari Window: A graphic model of interpersonal awareness. *Proceedings of the Western Training Laboratory in Group Development.* Los Angeles: UCLA.

Mamary, E, McCright, J and Roe, K (2007) Our lives: An examination of sexual health issues using Photovoice by non-gay identified African American men who have sex with men. *Culture, Health and Sexuality,* 9(4): 359–370.

Martin, H (2008) *Community Action and the Development of Social Capital in Glasgow's East End.* Submitted as MSc. Dissertation, The University of Glasgow.

Marx, K and Engels, F ([1845] 1998) *The German Ideology: Including Theses on Feuerbach and an Introduction to the Critique of Political Economy.* New York: Prometheus Books.

Mayo, M (1997) Partnerships for regeneration and community development: Some opportunities, challenges and constraints. *Critical Social Policy,* 52: 3–26.

Mayo, P (1999) *Gramsci, Freire and Adult Education.* London: Zed Books.

Mayo, P (2004) *Liberating Praxis: Paulo Freire's Legacy for Radical Education and Politics.* Westport, CT: Praeger.

McCormack, C (1993) From the Fourth to the Third World: A common vision of health. *Community Development Journal*, 28(3): 206–217.

McCowan, T (2003) Participation and education in the Landless People's Movement of Brazil. *Journal for Critical Education Policy Studies*, 1(1). Available at: **www.jceps.com/index.php?pageID=article& articleID=6** (accessed 13 November 2009).

McLaren, P (1998) *Life in Schools: An Introduction to Critical Pedagogy in the Foundations of Education*, 3rd ed. New York: Longman.

Merriam, SB and Kim, YS (2008) Non-Western perspectives on learning and knowing. *New Directions for Adult and Continuing Education*, 119: 71–81.

Mezirow, JD (1989) Transformation theory and social action: A response to Collard and law. *Adult Education Quarterly*, 39(2): 170–176.

Middleton, R (2002*) Studying Popular Music.* Philadelphia, PA: Open University Press.

Ministry of Education (1960) *The Youth Service in England and Wales ('The Albemarle Report').* London: HMSO.

Moorthy, R (undated) Rehearsal for reality. Available at: **www.pwynne.hostinguk.com/TIE%20and% 20Boal.htm** (accessed 13 November 2009).

Mutua, M (2002) *Human Rights: A Political and Cultural Critique.* Philadelphia, PA: University of Pennsylvania Press.

Noguera, P (2007) Renewing and reinventing Freire: A source of inspiration in inner-city youth education. In *Motion Magazine*, 16 October. Available at: **www.inmotionmagazine.com/er/pn_freire.html** (accessed 13 November 2009).

Norris, A (1997) 'Asylum': Theatre for Development in Oxford. *PLA Notes* 29: 50–51.

Olds, L (2007) Planning educational activities with eight overlapping and interlocking popular education principles. *Popular Education News.* Available at: **http://www.popednews.org/downloads/ planning_with_poped.pdf** (accessed 13 November 2009).

Parel, AJ (1997) *Gandhi: 'Hind Swaraj' and Other Writings.* Cambridge, Cambridge University Press.

PAULO (2003) *National Occupational Standards for Community Development Work.* Available at: **www.fcdl.org.uk/publications/documents/nos/Standards%20040703.pdf** (accessed 13 November 2009).

Picher, MC (undated) About the Theater of the Oppressed Laboratory. Available at: **www.toplab.org/lababout.htm** (accessed 13 November 2009).

Poulter, C (1995) Playing the (power) game. *Contemporary Theatre Review*, 3(1): 9–22.

Purcell, R (2005) *Working in the Community: Perspectives for Change.* Raleigh, NC: Lulu Press.

Purcell, R (2006) Lifelong learning and community: Social action, in Sutherland, P and Crowther, J (eds) *Lifelong Learning: Contexts and Concepts.* Abingdon: Routledge.

Putnam, RD (2001) *Bowling Alone: The Collapse and Revival of American Community*. New York: Simon & Schuster.

Rogers, C (1990) *The Carl Rogers Reader*. London: Constable.

Roy, A (1999) *The Cost of Living*. London: Flamingo.

Sainath, P (1999) *Everybody Loves a Good Drought*. London: Headline Books.

Santos, B (2008) Humanizing humanity: Theater of the Oppressed in prisons. *Under Pressure: The Newsletter of the International Theatre of the Oppressed*, 9(27). Available at: **www. theatreoftheoppressed.org/en/index.php?nodeID=33** (accessed 13 November 2009).

Selinger, E. (2008) Does microcredit 'empower'? Reflections on the Grameen Bank debate. *Human Studies*, 31(1): 27–41.

Sheehy, M and Warner, C (2001) *Partners Companion Manual to Training for Transformation*. Dublin: Partners.

Shor, I (1993) *Education is Politics: Paulo Freire's Critical Pedagogy*. New York: Routledge.

Smith, MK (1999, 2002) Youth work: An introduction. *The Encyclopedia of Informal Education*. Available at: **www.infed.org/youthwork/b-yw.htm** (accessed 13 November 2009).

Smith, MK and Doyle, ME (2002) The Albemarle Report and the development of youth work in England and Wales. *The Encyclopedia of Informal Education*. Available at: **www.infed.org/youthwork/ albemarle_report.htm** (accessed 13 November 2009).

Strinati, D (1995) *An Introduction to Theories of Popular Culture*. Routledge: London.

Thin, N (2002) *Social Progress and Sustainable Development*. London: ITGD Publishing.

Tuckman, BW and Jensen, MAC (1977) Stages of small group development revisited. *Group and Organizational Studies*, 2: 419–427.

Wang, CC and Burris, MA (1997) Photovoice: Concept, methodology, and use for participatory needs assessment. *Health Education and Behavior*, 24: 369–387.

Wang, CC, Morrel-Samuels, S, Hutchison, PM, Bell, L and Pestronk, RM (2004) Flint Photovoice: Community building among youths, adults, and policymakers. *American Journal of Public Health*, 94(6): 911–913.

Wilcox, D (1995) *The Guide to Effective Participation*. York: Joseph Rowntree Foundation.

Zimmerman, M (1995) Psychological empowerment: Issues and illustrations. *American Journal of Community Psychology*, 23: 581–600.

Index